P9-BYM-213

T R A N S M O N T A N U S

H I G H   S L A C K

Published by New Star Books

Series editor: Terry Glavin

Other books in the Transmontanus series

High Slack

Waddington's Gold Road and the Bute Inlet Massacre of 1864

Written and collected by *Judith Williams*

TRANSMONTANUS / NEW STAR BOOKS VANCOUVER

CONTENTS

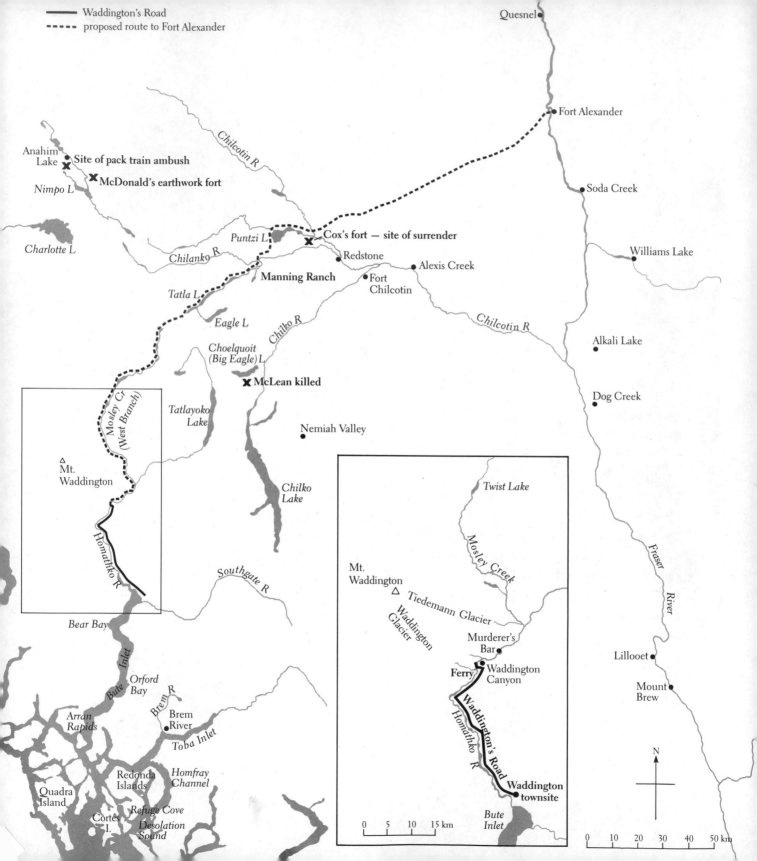

Part of the difficulty of this journey has been having to feel my way like this. I departed – my body deft, taut – with a clear image of where I should go: the route, the dangers, the distances by day. But then the landscape became vast.

Barry Lopez, FIELD NOTES

Homathko Valley, Bute Inlet, 20 kilometres upriver from Waddington's 'Half-Way Camp',
facing toward Waddington Glacier. The Homathko River is in the foreground.

PROLOGUE

Bute Wax

IN THE WINTER OF 1950, the handful of trappers and loggers resident in Bute Inlet reported that during extreme wind and temperature conditions, scow-loads of wax balls had rolled in great masses against the inlet's steep shores, opposite Bear Bay.

Bute Inlet, 120 miles northwest of Vancouver, is one of the largest fiords that have cut through the Coast Range batholith. For ten days, the wind had blown from the northeast, down the Homathko Valley from the great ice-fields around 13,260-foot Mount Waddington, and down the 48-mile channel. The temperature dropped to zero. Suddenly the wind direction turned, and long streaks of jelly-like matter began to collect around floating objects. The balls of wax grew up to eighteen inches in diameter.

Investigations revealed that quantities of waxy material had been seen in Bute Inlet, and at the mouth of Toba Inlet to the south, in 1922, then in December, 1935 and in January, 1936. Similar events were reported in February, 1950; March, 1951; November 1955; and in February and March, 1956.

A series of scientific expeditions has ascertained that as soon as the weather moderates, the wax balls melt into the water and their presence cannot be detected by chemical analysis. The mystery of the wax's storage is as great as its origin since the surface waters of the inlet are fresh, flow out, and are replaced by river water. Bute Inlet discharges into a complicated system of channels lying between the mainland and Vancouver Island at the north end of the Strait of Georgia. The channel depth varies from 1,000 to 2,200 feet, and its average width is two and a half miles. At the head of the Inlet, the Homathko and Southgate rivers form small, shifting deltas. The copious glacial run-offs from these rivers provide the inlet with a layer of fresh water, twenty to thirty feet deep.

Chemical analysis indicates that the substance closest to Bute Wax is the seed wax of the plant *Simmondsia chinenis*, which grows in California and Nevada. Searching for a possible plant material indigenous to Bute Inlet from which a similar material might be derived, scientists discovered that the mixture of fresh and salt water and the strong tidal and wind-currents discourage the growth of seaweeds and algae, and limit the source material to land plants.

In the spring of 1951, slicks of lodgepole pine pollen, up to 300 yards long, floated on the inlet near its head. In some years, this pollen forms such clouds over the inland valley that fires are mistakenly reported on the basis of the smoke-like mass. It has been suggested that the wax derives from this pollen, which floats downriver from the shores of backwaters where it was lodged in the early summer. From such resting places, it may be dislodged by the violent winds of the Homathko and Southgate valleys.*

* Adapted from M. Y. Richards in *Transactions* of the Royal Society of Canada, Vol. 51, Series 3, June, 1957.

The remains of Waddington's log boardwalk after a washout, Homathko Canyon, 1870s.

CHAPTER 1

Figures In Stone

REFUGE COVE, WEST REDONDA ISLAND, JULY 17, 1991 – I Am
unable to sleep tonight. Rising wind drags a bow across the strings of my
nerves as I turn over in my mind all the things I have learned about Bute
Inlet. The locals warn that the wind, known as a "Bute", is a very devil
and that the steep sides of the inlet provide no shelter past the Orford
River. Still, I want to set my feet down on the "gold road" Alfred
Waddington tried to build up the Homathko Valley, at the end of the
inlet, in the 1860s. My calmly sleeping husband, Bobo Fraser, has
agreed to come with me in our twenty-foot aluminum boat. I doze back
across the wake of my early explorations of the channels and inlets
between the Redonda Islands and the mainland.

SEPTEMBER 15, 1987 – Danny Louie, who was then chief of the
Klahoose Band, arrived at our dock in the *Klahoose I*. He and Sliammon
Chief Roy Francis wanted to inspect the effect of logging operations on
Indian reserve land in Toba Inlet. I was to point out the pictographs I
had discovered. We set out from Refuge into a glorious morning, intent
on spending the night at the head of the Inlet. Crossing Desolation
Sound northward into Homfray Channel was like skating through a
mirror.

Joe Barnes, an 83-year-old elder who had been raised at the Tahumming River, was along to provide direction and context. When we stopped at the first pictograph ledge in Homfray he said: "The paint comes from the sea, up there in Toba. I saw the pictures first when I was six. Danny's great-grandfather said he'd seen them when he was young, but nobody knew their stories."

Pigment is still there, ground into the stone palette below a man, outlined in red, arm outstretched, who appears to ride – a canoe? "No, look!" – a monster head, in stone, marked with a red eye and joined with a few strokes to a back and body bulged out of stone. "It's a dragon, or a serpent, with feet." His painted companion on the ledge is solid red, big belly, hands the size of mine, quiffs of hair on end, somehow in charge. My forefinger traces red fish entering a circle, man in a boat for sure, and a fishy cousin to the seawolves at Petroglyph Park. According to the chart, the water between here and Ahpokum is up to 399 fathoms deep, and Mount Addenbroke rises abruptly 5,215 feet at our backs. Across the channel, Mount Denman's never-glaciated peak is 6,590 feet high. The water is electric, green and cold. Wonder place: wilderness and abyss. "Dad tells stories of a Homfray Channel sea-serpent," Danny says. The pictures snap into focus, are no longer arbitrary.

Whatever marks the mind has made in this wilderness, the stone has absorbed into itself. The mystery of this absorption was solved by observing that a translucent whitish substance bound the paint to the stone in a kind of fresco process. The stone galleries were carefully chosen to be white, lidded stages. Red oxide, burnt to intensify its colour, was bound with salmon eggs that become adhesive beyond expectation when mixed with saliva. Milky calcrite or silicate, released in minute amounts by the rain, fixed the images and the alkaline surface slowed the growth of lichen. If too much calcrite accrued, or the overhang was insufficient, the paint blurred. If the flow persisted, it could bury the paintings, and they would be visible or not depending on the moisture content of the air, or the angle of light.

The paintings, made for the act of making, are both event and its residue, not to be "looked at" as though they were "pictures" of things, but to mark a connection that had occurred, some spirit of place recognized. When I flip back and forth visually, between image and ground, my shifting from the substance of the rock to a red image emphasizes the embedding of human activity in natural systems. All petroglyph or pictograph sites occur where human and geographical energy meet. So potent is this ledge that each subsequent visit has been preceded by a search in a nearby tree for the "Michelin man", formed – of what? a wasp's nest, crystalized pitch, or ambitious fungus? The pneumatic form is hung between a rock painting of a whale and this rock stage onto which, at high slack, we can walk straight off the boat. At certain times the ledge has burned with a lattice of light cast up from the sea, and image, mass and me are consumed in a perfection of being in place.

Some rock art sites are so powerful as to be recognizable while going flat out in a speed boat. Once, I yelled "Stop!" and we turned and came face to face with an enormous being, all teeth and grimace, so old a painting it *is* covered with a stubble of lichen. To one side, a ritual pool. An archeological excavation at the site, I later learned, revealed 9,000 years of occupation of that island.

On the *Klahoose I*, we crossed the channel to Ahpokum. The native names to the area are a code of usage. Ahpokum means "having maggots", and refers to the cliff at the left entrance of the bay. The colour of milt, or spawned-out salmon flesh, the cliff is said to turn whiter when the salmon have decided that sufficient rain has filled the spawning creeks. Once, I saw a 40-pound white spring salmon caught where the Forbes River forks, past native fish traps, into the green bay.

On the mainland shore, high up on a second ledge under Mount Denman, is the skeletal figure of a man, red on a luminous ground. A shaman balanced on one foot, a vandal's bullet through his heart. In the 1930s Klahoose Chief Julian identified this figure as Quodham, who had lived 350 years before.

Bob Dominic, an elder from Tork, the Klahoose village at Squirrel Cove, tried to teach me how to pronounce Tu7kw. Asked about the pictographs I had seen, he recalled: "My Mother said you don't go there. It's not because of wild animals, it … "

I prompted, too quickly: "Sacred?"

"Yes," he answered. "Spirits."

As the *Klahoose I* passed from Homfray Channel to Brem Bay and turned up Toba Inlet, the jade sea was calm, the cascades spectacular. The Inlet takes its name from the Spanish, Canal de la Tabla, so named by the Spanish naval officers Dionisio Alcala Galiano and Don Cayento Valdés because on June 27, 1792 they found here a *tabla* of planks. By a Spanish chart engraver's error, "Tabla" became "Toba". The atlas of the first edition of the *Relacion del Viage Hecho por las Goletas Sutil y Mexicana, 1792* reproduces the sketch of the *tabla* done on the spot by the young José Cardero. The eight-foot by five-foot panel, painted with what Valdes called "geometric and realistic figures", was perhaps a grave marker or, like the old dance screens from the west coast of Vancouver Island, announced territorial ownership. The stubby animals are possibly the mountain goats important to Klahoose people. Over the head of the central skeletized figure is a series of radiating lines, like those depicting individuals engaged in spirit quests in pictographs and petroglyphs throughout the world.

Valdes' *Mexicana* and the *Sutil* were, like Captain George Vancouver's ships *Discovery* and *Chatham*, en route to Nootka Sound on the west coast of Vancouver Island. Their mission was to resolve the "Nootka controversy" between the Spanish and the British over which of them had possession of the area – despite the 10,000-year occupation by the people of the area. The explorers had met south of Point Grey and agreed to pool information, but the Spanish, irritated by Vancouver's insistence that the British remap Toba Inlet themselves, didn't tell them about the existence of the *tabla*. Unwell, Vancouver remained on board the *Discovery* at Teakerne Arm, on West Redonda Island, working on his charts. "Our situation here," he wrote in his log, "is totally desolate." Hence Desolation Sound. But the sailors brewed up spruce beer and, according to Menzies, the ship's doctor, used the lake above Teakerne Falls "as a resort". Desolation Sound indeed!

Diagonally across the channel from the sole island in the inlet, where anthropologist Erna Gunther says the *tabla* was found, a bare rock face

A contemporary engraving of the 'tabla' from which Toba Inlet takes its name.

rises over 3,500 feet directly from the water. We were enjoined by Joe Barnes not to look too closely at a vast, malignant weeping face on the cliff. To point at Cowhŭn would cause rain, or raise winds. At the Tahumming River, Joe led us up to a huge cedar cross rising out of the salal. Graves sank and yawned under cedar hearts and crosses. Joe, Danny and Roy found the names of their ancestors. A stone slab, with stone finger raised, bore the words "Moses, 1888"; on a marble obelisk, swathed in real and carved ivy, was carved: "Julius of Toba, born 1815, died 1905."

As one travels upcoast, across the sounds and into the maze of islands and iron canyons, the values one brings flourish, then fade. The hours are ruled by sun, wind and tide. One should not be too comfortable, nor take one's life along. At some point, it is necessary to give over to the journey.

Standing on the white shell middens of ancient villages, time winds round like a moon snail shell, voices echo and currents plug in. Such was the effect of a series of trips that I now undertook through space and telescoping time, that I returned from each journey enchanted. Since then I have searched for ways to manifest "charts," textual and visual, with which to navigate these dimensions simultaneously. Space means moving through, over, the distance between. Time widens around direction in a spiral. To move in both dimensions I need to know the human event as well as the geological and geographical facts.

Consulting Captain John T. Walbran's *British Columbia Coast Names: 1592-1906*, I discovered: "Homfray Channel: Desolation Sound. After Robert Homfray, civil engineer, residing in Victoria, 1860-1902. Born 1824. Native of Hales Owen, Worcestershire … arrived from California in 1860 and was engaged in surveying duties … He was of an eccentric disposition, and for some years before his death he had his tombstone erected in Ross Bay Cemetery, with all particulars on it with the exception of the date of his decease."

For Doris Hope, doyenne of the Refuge Cove Oral History Society since St Patrick's Day, 1943, the name Homfray Creek provoked this response: "One hundred and eighty men."

She lit a cigarette, put her foot up and settled in.

"One hundred and eighty men worked there logging in 1945. The loggers came to our dock at Refuge on the Union Steamships and Dorothy's and Ed's camp boat ran them up to Homfray. A boatman would pick them up and transport them to the bunkhouses. One day I looked out and saw a young woman on the float getting into Ed's boat. She was all done up. Summer frock, high-heeled shoes, my dear, stockings, hat, the lot! At Homfray, she tried to balance clean in the greasy skiff and the boatman …"

"Drunk?"

"Undoubtedly. The boatman revved up the engine – those haywire old boats – you don't know! He revved it up and when he looked around she was, the woman was, bare in her pants and bra, the dress sucked clean off her by the drive belt. The bastard sat right here telling the story.

AMOR DE COSMOS: *Editor of the* British Colonist, *later premier of British Columbia, 1872-74. Changed his name from William Smith to 'lover of the cosmos'.*

'God damn it,' he said. 'Damn if I'd only just revved it up a little higher.' 'You wouldn't.' 'I would. I could have gotten it all off her.' "

Jim Spilsbury, radio wizard and pioneer airline operator, makes a yearly visit to Doris, his sister-in-law, at Refuge. When I asked him about Homfray Creek, he instructed: "Don't cut shakebolts above a waterfall."

"In Homfray Creek, my cousin and I, the summer of '24, cut bolts up over the falls, and shakebolts, believe me, when sent over such falls, can fly pretty far into the woods or spill out into a channel and float away. Our summer's work. I was nineteen."

Jim held up a box to fix my eyes and told of how he had come by a paper bag of copper bracelets, payment for mending a broken radio owned by a destitute logger who, he later learned, robbed graves. I circled copper up and down my arms, and I never took/take/turned off that current to the past.

My grandmother's old dictionary calls a channel "a bed of water or navigable waterway, a course in which anything moves, a route, a furrow or groove, a frequency band."

Searching another kind of geography – the murky depths of microfiche – I found Robert Homfray's record of his journey up Bute Inlet in the winter of 1861 to survey a route for Alfred Waddington's road to the Cariboo gold fields. Around Homfray's account collected a mass of images, stories and journeys, then newspaper reports of smallpox. Suddenly, in 1864, the record dead-ends just above the Homathko Canyon and explodes into the event known as the Chilcotin War. This archival landscape details the evolution of the province of British Columbia from the newcomers' point of view. One navigates through connecting channels of fact, rumour and decidedly subjective opinion. One stands, stunned, at intersections. The *British Colonist*, Victoria's main newspaper, begun by Amor de Cosmos in 1858, was awash in romantic hyperbole, enthusiastic self-interest, and cries of "Lo the poor Indian," but some facts seem reliable.

On June 22, 1859, Robert Homfray reports for duty, in his good-schoolboy hand, to Captain Parsons of the Victoria Royal Engineers. In 1861,

the *Colonist* reports him as returning in some disarray from Bute Inlet. On August 8, 1869, he mounts a telescope in a Victoria alley in order to view the "Great Solar Eclipse". He orders a dragger to rake the Victoria harbour area so he can add to his collection of shells. When we last hear from him, he is engaged in a dispute with the dean of Christ Church Cathedral over his intention to erect the red granite ball that is his tombstone before his death. He died, single, on September 19, 1902.

I have assumed that the tale he published in the *Victoria Province*, in 1894, was created from a book Homfray mentions rescuing when a canoe was destroyed. I have not been able to find the original journal.

To recreate Homfray's diary, I have taken December 20, 1861 (which the *British Colonist* reports as the date of Homfray's return to Victoria) and the fact that Homfray is reported to have been away two months, and invented a set of dates for the story as he tells it.

Robert Homfray, fifth from left holding a cornet, in front of the old Legislative Building, Victoria, 1866, with other members of the Royal Volunteer Rifle Corps Band.

Hudson's Bay Fort Camosun, Victoria, 1858.

CHAPTER 2

A Winter Journey in 1861

BY ROBERT HOMFRAY

In November 1857, the *Active*, a schooner-rigged paddle steamer, was engaged with the *Plumper* in Semiahmoo Bay fixing the position of the 49th parallel. While there a white man named Macaulay, who had been illicitly supplying intoxicants, was made a prisoner and the *Active* conveyed him to Esquimalt. On the way Macaulay showed the crew a large quantity of gold dust which he had received in trade from the Fraser River Indians. The crew on arrival at San Francisco the following winter spread the news, and the gold rush to the Fraser River was the result.

– Personal reminiscence from Charles Holtz, who served on board the *Active*, 1854-58, to Captain John T. Walbran

VICTORIA, BRITISH COLUMBIA, OCTOBER 18, 1861 – It was in the Hudson's Bay Company's Fort at Victoria, in October, that an exploring party was formed by the above company, at the instigation of Mr. Waddington, a relative of the late French Ambassador to the British Court. He arrived early in 1858, the year of the gold discoveries in British Columbia, from San Francisco, to see if it was possible to transport goods from Victoria by way of Bute Inlet across the Chilcotin Plains to

* The Coast Range was in those
days referred to as the Cascade
Range.

Harry McNeill

the rich gold fields of Cariboo, by a shorter route than that of the Fraser River, and to find out if a wagon road could be made from the head of Bute Inlet along the Howathco River and through the Cascade Range.*

The Hudson's Bay Company asked me to take charge of the expedition. I consented although some of the company's officers warned me not to go, telling me I would not come back alive, that it was madness to attempt it in the middle of such a severe winter. They also pointed out the great danger of navigating the Gulf of Georgia for so long a distance in a frail canoe, on to the head of Bute Inlet, up an unknown river, and through an unknown country among mountains covered with snow, surrounded by fierce and savage tribes who had never seen a white man, besides the great risk of being buried under avalanches, attacked by hungry wolves, not to mention the ever to be dreaded grizzly, with the off chance of perishing miserably in the snow from starvation and exposure.

All these things, and more also, were pointed out to me. It certainly was not very cheering information: but distance lends enchantment to the view, and having a great desire to see new and strange sights, and being possessed of a fair amount of courage, I determined to go. The Hudson's Bay Company sent their three best French Canadian voyageurs, Coté, Balthazzar, and Bourchier, with Harry McNeill and two Indians, so that including myself our party consisted of seven all told. Coté was appointed in charge of the party as long as we are on the water, as he best understood the management of a canoe, and I was appointed captain when on land. I took a book with me in which I recorded the daily events. Our outfit consisted of one canoe, two tents, two muskets and ammunition to supply ourselves with food on the way and for protection; two blankets each, two axes, one hatchet, one spade and a small supply of provisions on account of our having to pack them on our backs through the snow after we left the canoe; also some beads and trinkets as presents for the Indians in order that they might deal kindly with us while we were passing through their territory.

OCTOBER 24 – The weather was fine the day we left Victoria. We camped at night and left early in the morning. It blew hard next day with a heavy sea, making our canoe leak, which we had to repair after every gale. On account of the rough weather it took us several days before we ran through the rapids to camp above Nanaimo, near the place where we proposed to cross the Gulf in the morning.

The morning was fine although the appearance of the Gulf was far from encouraging.

When we were nearly half way across it the wind began to blow, and it looked as though a severe storm would overtake us before we could reach the opposite side of the Gulf. Several whales crossed our bow which frightened us very much. Our canoe was often buried in the waves; however, we finally succeeded in reaching the opposite shore, our canoe leaking badly.

OCTOBER 25 – Five days out from Victoria we reached Texada Island at sunset. After we left next day we were almost lost in the heavy seas; when we landed to repair our canoe a deer passed us with a large wolf in full chase.

OCTOBER 30 – In nine days we were in the entrance of Bute Inlet,* three miles wide, snow-covered mountains on both sides, rising almost perpendicularly 1,000 feet from the water.

It blew a hurricane at night and the noise was like the roar of a cataract. We could hear the avalanches coming down the sides of the mountains. It had been snowing heavily up above for several days.

NOVEMBER 1 – We met Indians coming down the inlet in four canoes lashed together with poles across them. They had a cargo of dried salmon, and had built a platform three feet above the canoe and on which they lived. When they saw us they made for the shore and landed their women and children, who ran up the rocks. The Indians in their canoes then came straight at us with levelled muskets. Our two Indians made signs to them not to fire. We were very greatly alarmed. At last we succeeded in allaying their fears and came along side them and made them presents of beads, etc., when they allowed us to pass on.

NOVEMBER 2 – Next day we saw a large canoe coming directly to us

* According to Homfray's later notes, and newspaper reports, his route was past Texada and Savary Islands, across the mouth of Malaspina Inlet, into Desolation Sound, and up the channel between East Redonda Island and the mainland. It was only after being taken to the Klahoose chief's village that they went up Bute Inlet.

from a dark chasm in the mountains across the inlet, paddling hard. We regarded it with suspicion, and as the canoe came near to us, Coté called out to McNeill, "Down with the sail! Down with the sail!"

One of the Indians who was sitting behind me was so frightened that he fired his musket in the air. It startled us all very much as we thought we were being attacked by some other canoe in the rear. As they came nearer we could see six half-naked Indians, each with a musket in the canoe.

They came alongside, seized our canoe, and one of them jumped into it, the others held on to the sides, and we were completely overpowered.

They pointed to the chasm in the mountains that they had just left, and made signs to us to paddle hard. None of us spoke but quietly resigned ouselves to certain death. As we came near the shore there were deep mutterings among the half-naked Indians, and they picked up their muskets and were just landing.

We now expected that our end had come, when suddenly we heard a loud war-whoop sounding across the water and repeated several times.

There was great commotion amongst those Indians when they heard it, and they hesitated to carry out their murderous resolve. On looking behind us we saw a tall powerful Indian standing in his canoe waving his paddles in the air and calling out loudly. He was coming quickly toward us: we got out of the canoe and stood, shoulder to shoulder, on the beach determined to die together. We had only two empty muskets.

On his approaching the shore the six Indians jumped into their canoe and made off.

He then told our two Indians that he was the chief of the powerful Cla-oosh tribe, and those six Indians belonged to a distant tribe, who lived entirely on plundering and killing any person they met in a solitary canoe, and to our great joy our lives were saved.

He then took us up a river to his encampment for we were very weak and exhausted, and he fed us on mountain sheep, beaver, and bear meat and was very kind to us and we made him many presents of beads and trinkets.

NOVEMBER 5 – I told our Indians to ask him if he knew of any trail through the mountains and his answer was "Yes, but that it was covered with snow and ice and very dangerous to travel over, and that no Indians ever venture there on account of the grizzly bears that at this time of year were very ferocious." We offered him many presents if he would only come with us to show us the entrance to the pass through the mountains, as we were most anxious to survey the country, and at last he consented to go with us.

NOVEMBER 8 – The weather was clear and freezing hard. He often warned us to be on the lookout for the marauding Indians, who had taken us prisoners, and to be careful to put out the campfire at night.

NOVEMBER 10 – At the head of Bute Inlet we camped where an immense slide had come down from a very high peak, leaving in its course for half a mile a snow embankment of great height, carrying immense boulders, trees etc., with it into the Inlet. The tops of high pine trees growing near the side of the slide were just visible above the top of the avalanche.

NOVEMBER 11 – The Indian chief now took us up the Howathco River, and pointed to a peak a long distance off where the river comes through a canyon in the mountains.

NOVEMBER 12 – Close by us was an immense glacier. We made a deep hole in the ground and buried some of our provisions, and covered them with logs and dirt and snow on top, so as to ensure a supply in case of accident on a return trip. We now began our upriver journey.

NOVEMBER 13 – After a time it became full of dangerous rapids. We tied a long rope to the canoe, two men pushing it up the rapids with poles, the rest of us on shore hauling on the rope.

NOVEMBER 14 – At last we came to a large *embarras* formed of drifted logs piled on top of each other by the winter floods – about twenty feet high and half a mile long, stretching across the river, and the water surging between the logs with great velocity. We had a dangerous task to perform as we had to lift the canoe over into the water on the other side. The logs were very slippery and covered with snow, and any

THE KLAHOOSE (TL'ÚHUS OR CLA-OOSH) PEOPLE: *Occupied territory in Toba Inlet, Homfray Channel, and Ramsay Arm. They moved to Cortes Island in the late 1800s.*

mis-step would have precipitated us into the raging torrent. We dug a deep hole in the snow and pitched our tent inside, the wind blowing continually with great violence down the river toward the Inlet. The noise of the avalanches falling night and day was deafening.

NOVEMBER 15 – It snowed hard; wolves and bear tracks were constantly seen on both sides of the river. A little further on we saw a dead grizzly bear, which was being devoured by several large vultures perched on the carcass. The salmon were frozen in the ice on the river sides, and we took them up in our hands; they were alive although coated over with ice. We saw two black bears standing on their hind legs looking at us from the river bank, probably wondering where we were bound for.

NOVEMBER 17 – The Indian chief at last advised us to turn back; he said he would go no further with us, and that if we went on we would be lost. We consulted together to see what we had better do, and we thought it would show great want of courage if we did not go on although our clothes were fast wearing out.

The Indian chief then left us, waded across the river and disappeared in the bush, our efforts to pursuade him having proved unavailing.

NOVEMBER 18 – We sighted a grand peak at least 7,000 feet high in the distance, glittering in the sunlight, covered with an eternal mantle of snow, and saw several mountain sheep on the rocks, also beaver dams in the river with beavers outside keeping guard. The water was getting so shallow that we were continually polling and hauling on the rope, wading in the icy water, and pushing the canoe along with our hands, all of us tied together with a long line, each having a pole in his hands to sound the river for fear of getting out of our depth. Several times we were nearly lost in the rapids.

NOVEMBER 19 – We saw a fine glacier completely filling up a valley several miles in length from the mountain tops, and breaking off at the edge of the river, with a perpendicular side a hundred feet thick of the most beautiful blue colour, crested over with glistening white snow.

Our two Indians supplied us with mountain sheep, beaver and deer, which they have shot. The wild animals make a frightful noise at night, coming close down to the bank, being nearly starved, their only food being the frozen salmon. Traces of where they had eaten the salmon on the river bank were visible by the blood marks on the snow.

NOVEMBER 20 – The river was now full of rapids, 13 feet rise in 100 feet, and intensely cold. At last the tow rope broke and the canoe shot down the rapids like an arrow, and we had the most infinite difficulty in recovering it. The men were almost lost, and we found it quite impossible to proceed in the canoe any further. We saw now when too late that we should have followed the Indian chief's advice and turned back with him. We could now see the great canyon in the distance where the river came through the Mountains but how we were going to get there we could not tell.

NOVEMBER 21 – We buried the canoe in the snow and determined to walk along the river banks. Tied together as we were and with our sounding poles in our hands we had to wade the river several times in the day as it was so crooked. The ice formed on our clothes as we came out of the water, it was so bitterly cold. We packed only a blanket each and some food, for we were too weak to carry the tent. The river boulders, coated with ice, give the appearance of huge glass balls. Our beards and moustaches were continually frozen together, so we can scarcely open our mouths. For some time past we had been unable to wash as the water froze instantly on our faces and hair. The mountains were covered in a dazzling sheet of snow. Coté cheered us up with the hope that we might come across foot tracks, as he thought that our only hope to escape from miserable death lay in falling in with Indians.

NOVEMBER 24 – Very soon after as we were going round a point of rocks, I saw the tracks of a moccasin in the snow. We kept close together in single file, one musket in front and one in the rear. Suddenly we saw a tall powerful Indian and his squaw standing on the river edge, looking cautiously about, having evidently heard us.

Directly they saw us, the woman ran behind the man who was nearly naked, his body was painted jet black with large vermilion-coloured rings around his eyes. He had a bow and arrow in his hand which he presented at us. He danced up and down in a stooping position with his knees bent, uttering frightful sounds.

We stood still, Coté telling us to lay our heads on our shoulders and close our eyes to show him that we wanted to sleep; then to open and shut our mouths so that he might see we were hungry and wished to make friends with him. We advanced toward him a few steps at a time and halted when we were near. Not fearing anything, I went slowly up to him, when he seized me in his arms, and I was helpless in his powerful embrace. Coté ran up saying: "Don't fear Sir, he shan't kill you."

The Indian then slackened his hold, lifted up my arms, looked into my mouth and examined my ears, to see if I was made like himself, as he had evidently never seen a white man before. Eventually he made up his mind that we were friendly and that we wanted somewhere to sleep. He pointed toward the canyon and made a sketch in the snow with his arrow, waving his arms for us to go up the river. We now felt certain there were other Indians not far off. Some distance further, on rising ground, we suddenly saw several Indians coming up out of different holes in the ground, which startled us very much. We stood still and repeated the motions we had gone through before. They too had bows and arrows and danced their defiant war dance. Then, one of their number, who was apparently their chief, came, with a slow and dignified step, a few paces towards us, the others covering him with their bows and arrows, then he walked backwards, with his face towards us, and hung something of a red colour on a bush and stood still. We then went slowly up to them. They examined us carefully from head to foot and made signs for us to go down the holes they came out of. We were so terrified that they might kill us once they had got us down, that for a long time we refused to go. However, knowing that we were entirely in their power we at last decided to follow them into their holes. Coté asked me if I would go down with him leaving the others on guard outside with their muskets. I agreed to go down with him and the chief led the way.

We followed him on our hands and knees into his underground den, which was a place about ten feet square and about eight feet deep. When we got inside we saw a very old squaw and her daughter. They had a small fire burning.

We had only been down a few minutes and warming our hands at the flames when we heard the report of a musket, Coté calling to me to come quickly as the Indians were killing those we left outside on guard. When we got out we were greatly relieved to be told that the musket had accidentally gone off in the hands of one of our Indians. Fortunately, the muzzle was pointed upwards and no one was hurt. Not one of the natives was to be seen; they had been so terribly frightened at the sudden report that they had all disappeared underground. Shortly after we all went down into the hole where the chief and his squaw lived. She was very old and shrivelled and almost blind with a face the colour of mahogany, her hair matted with dirt and grease. We took with us a small piece of bread that we had made at our last camp fire, and we offered them some, they refused to eat until we consumed some first. The old lady seemed pleased. She then took down a wooden dish and held it to the fire-light to see if it was clean but her eyes were so dim with age that she was not satisfied with it. She then began spitting in it several times and wiped it out with her hair. She then opened one of the Indian boxes and emptied the contents into the dish. The smell from the contents was indescribably overpowering; it might have been the fermented entrails of some animal. Coté told us that we must eat all of it, as it was in her opinion the choicest food she had to offer and it was a token of her friendly feeling toward us. We all said we could not eat it; he said we must or they might in all probability do us some harm when asleep.

She handed me the dish. It was fortunate that being so old and blind that she could not see us when we gave the contents of the dish to the Indian dogs lying behind us. We nodded to her and smiled and she thought we had eaten it. The chief then came down and we made signs that we wanted to sleep. We took it in turns to watch while the others slept.

Next morning we made signs to them and pointing in the direction of the canyon they understood that we wished to know if there was a trail that way. They made sketches with a stick on the snow and pointing their hands to the sun and moving it slowly from east to west several times made us understood that after many days the sun would melt the ice and snow and then we would be able to go through the canyon. They made signs for us to go back where we came from. We gave them all the beads and trinkets we had left. They gave us some dried salmon. They would not let us stay the remainder of the winter with them as they have but little to eat themselves.

NOVEMBER 25 – So, weary and footsore and our clothes nearly worn out, we began our homeward journey, hardly caring what befell us on the way, as it seemed impossible that we could reach the Inlet alive.

These were the same Indians who about three years afterwards killed fourteen out of sixteen white men belonging to Mr. Waddington's road party. I met one of the two men who escaped the massacre and he told me how it was done. He and the others were all fast asleep when suddenly on a dark night the Indians crept up silently and cut all the tent ropes. The tents then fell down on the poor men sleeping underneath. The Indians each had previously taken one of the white men's axes, and when they saw any man struggling to get out from underneath they struck their axes through the tent, killing many of them at a single blow. The cries of the wounded were heart-rending, but all was soon over. The two who escaped laid perfectly still, being afraid to stir. The two men crept out and jumped into the river, swimming to the opposite side and escaped to another camp of white men several miles further down. They all immediately left for Bute Inlet and went down to Victoria. The people were horror-stricken on hearing of so shocking a massacre; and a proclamation was immediately issued by Mr. Seymour, the Governor of British Columbia, calling for volunteers to go up and bring down the Indians, dead or alive, to trial. Nerely 150 men, including many Indians, headed by Governor Seymour himself with several Magistrates, went up and chased the Indians through the mountains. Some were killed, some escaped and the others were captured, tried and hanged. Several white men of the party were also killed.

This terrible massacre was caused by the ill-treatment of the Indian women by Mr. Waddington's party who were making the road.

NOVEMBER 27 – As for us we managed to reach the place where we had buried the canoe, tent etc., in the snow. Navigating the canoe now became very dangerous, the river being full of rapids, the canoe shooting down the stream with great rapidity. By and by we got into the wrong channel and our poles breaking we were swept under the branches of several trees and nearly swamped.

We were fortunate to witness a grand sight just after sunrise. On the opposite side of the river, nearly half a mile from us we heard a sharp crash and then a loud rumbling sound high up on a mountain directly in view. The entire side of the mountain for fully a mile in length was in motion. A huge avalanche came thundering down with a frightful noise, pine trees going down before it like a swath of mown grass; it lasted several minutes, the ground sensibly shaking from the violence of the shock, and enormous masses of rock came crashing down into the valley below. Immediately it was over dense clouds of steamy vapour arose, caused by the heat from the friction of the immense masses of rock grinding and crushing against each other in their descent and their contact with the snow and wet earth was the cause of this steamy vapour.

Very soon after, in a bend in the river, the Indians suddenly cried out in alarm as the canoe was dashed, bow on, against a large tree lying across the river. One of the broken limbs of the tree pierced the canoe and held it fast; the water instantly rushing in, we all quickly got out on the tree and seized some blankets, part of a sack of flour, two tents, three iron pots, musket, my note-book, the spade and some matches and carried them along the tree on to the bank. We then discovered to our horror that our two axes were in the bow of the canoe. After great difficulty we succeeded in getting them out; everything else was swept away. The bottom of the canoe had fallen out and only the sides remained. The

Indians were crying and beating sticks together saying they would never see their children again. We were thankful that our lives are saved, but what was now to become of us God only knew. It was a very long way to where the Indians lived in Desolation Sound, perhaps 90 miles distant, and no other way of reaching them except by water; and our canoe being lost, death seemed to stare us in the face.

We boiled some flour, making a dish of the spade; no spoons, no tea or coffee, the weather bitterly cold and the snow very deep.

NOVEMBER 29 – We had now to make a raft to carry us down river to where we had buried some few provisions at the head of the inlet. We cut down some dried timber and tied them together with cedar bark. Two of them sank and the other would only bear the weight of two men, and there were seven of us.

Coté and one Indian volunteered to go on the raft; the rest of us had to wade through deep snow along the river bank. Coté saying that the two on the raft might be lost and those who walked along the bank might be saved. We were afraid that some Indians might have seen us burying the provisions and had stolen them.

NOVEMBER 30 – On the fourth day after we lost the canoe we arrived at the "cache" to find our provisions intact at which we greatly rejoiced. We all ate with our fingers – the knives and spoons having gone down with the canoe and all of us had to drink out of one baking powder tin. Despite our cache I put us all on very short allowances.

We were now at the head of Bute Inlet and very weak from cold and exposure, our clothes continually freezing as we waded through the many streams. We were in hopes that we might see some Indians who could take us in their canoes but there were none to be seen. All our hopes of safety had vanished.

Our only hope was to cut down a tree and on it float down the inlet some 70 miles to Desolation Sound.

DECEMBER 1 – The wind had been blowing seven days and nights with heavy snow storm and we were in great danger from the falling timber. We were attacked by 12 hungry wolves, who came boldly at us out of the bush, snapping and barking. We ran and pulled fire brands out of the fire and threw them at them but it was some time before they were driven off.

Bourchier and the Indians often cried, which made us all miserable. Coté said I was the bravest man in the party.

DECEMBER 9 – The first two trees we cut down split in falling, the next, 30 feet long, seemed alright. It took us 10 days to cut a long hollow in it 18" wide as we had but two blunt axes to work with. We rolled it some little distance to the water and then nearly everyone refused to get on it. The men said they would sooner die on land than be drowned. Eventually, however, they were persuaded, and we got on it with our things.

Being nearly round on the bottom it rolled a good deal; and we all agreed that if it turned over, we would go down together, as there was no possibility of our clinging to the sides of the perpendicular rocky inlet. Several times we nearly rolled over. We seldom spoke to each other expecting every minute to go down.

At last we reached a place where we could land; it was here we had to cross the inlet, three miles wide. We felt certain it would be extremely dangerous for all of us to cross on the log. Four was as many as it could safely carry, and if it should begin to blow those who were on it would surely be lost and the other three who were left on land would perish in the snow. We had half a bag of flour left, one musket, a little powder and a few bullets. We all shook hands as we parted, never expecting to see each other again.

Coté and three others went on the log. I and two others remained here in the snow. Soon after they started to cross they held up part of a flour sack as a sail; the log was going very steadily, having now only four men on it. We eagerly watched them until they disappeared under the shadow of the mountain on the opposite side. The intention was for Coté with those on the log to proceed to Desolation Sound and induce the Indians to come to our rescue. He thought he would get back in about ten days.

DECEMBER 11 – We were now afraid that the six half-naked Indians who had taken us prisoners before might find us, and had perhaps already killed Coté and the others who went on the log. Bourchier was always crying for his family. I cheered him up as well as I could.

One morning Balthazzar had gone up the mountain close by to see if he could shoot a deer; and for fear that those six Indians might be prowling around we erected a screen made of bark and hid behind it. It was a clear bright morning and Bourchier was on the watch; he suddenly espied a dark spot on the water a long distance off. He was sure it was those six Indians, as Coté had not had time to get back; he was greatly distressed. I told him to cheer up and be brave. Half and hour later we saw it was a canoe coming straight at us about a mile off. He said, "Shall I call Balthazzar down from the mountain?" I said, "No, they will hear you." They were paddling hard; we could see one tall Indian standing up in the bow of the canoe. Presently we heard a loud war-whoop sounding along the water. Our death seemed now certain; a cold perspiration came over me; neither of us spoke. A short time after another war whoop sounded louder and longer than before; we resigned ourselves to our fate. By and by to our great joy we heard Coté call out and we thanked God we were all saved. Coté foolishly frightened us by telling the Indian to utter his war cry. He was the Cla-oosh chief who rescued us from the Indians and piloted us up the river and tried to induce us to go back with him, but we foolishly insisted on going on. Coté met the Indians before reaching Desolation Sound and returned with them sooner than he expected.

DESOLATION SOUND, DECEMBER 13 – The Cla-oosh chief brought us safely to Desolation Sound where his tribe lived, and we stayed with him until they had dried their salmon. It was intensely cold all the time.

DECEMBER 14 – The Indians seemed satisfied when I told them that if they would take me to Victoria we would give them many blankets and muskets. They said their canoes were almost too small to cross the Gulf in winter time. However, they provided us with two canoes; six of their Indians went in one canoe, ourselves in the other. They were very kind to us and seemed sorry that were going away.

DECEMBER 17 – A day or two after we left the sea became very rough and we had to put in several times. The Indians were continually watching the drifting clouds, calling us up at any time in the night when there was a chance to get away.

This was necessary; the canoes were so small it is dangerous to run any risk in rough seas, especially as we saw several whales passing near us.

DECEMBER 18 – At last we came to where the Indians proposed to cross the Gulf. But when we were half way across it became very rough; we all thought it was impossible to reach the other side. The canoes were often buried in the waves, but Providence was watching over us and we were very thankful to reach the opposite shore near Nanaimo.

When within half a mile of the Narrows the tide was running out very strong and as we came in sight of them we saw to our great alarm two whales in front of the centre of the Narrows with their heads toward us. The water there is very shallow and the tide was running with such a powerful race that they appeared unable to move out of our way. We were going very fast with the tide, the water white with foam; it seemed impossible for us to escape coming into collision with their bodies. The Indians shouted and waved their paddles but to no purpose as they did not move, and we shot past between them about 50 or 60 feet from the nearest one and were in the rapids a moment after.

DECEMBER 20 – After a few days we came past Cadboro Bay where the Indians caught sight of some cows. They immediately stopped paddling and would not go on for several minutes and, making loud noises, appeared very much astonished, having never seen any animal of the kind before. As we passed Beacon Hill they again ceased paddling, making louder noises than before at the sight of some persons on horseback.

When we reached the Hudson's Bay Company's wharf, we could scarcely prevail on them to come ashore; they saw many strange Indians near them and were afraid. They had never seen a town and the different objects they saw were new and strange to them. Presently a horse

Victoria, 1862.

and cart came down the wharf and when they saw the horse coming near them they clung to us trembling, afraid to come further for a considerable time. Soon a number of people surrounded us. Mr. Findlayson, Dr. Tolmie, and Mr. Waddington came shortly after. Everyone was glad to see we were safe back again. They were surprised to see us in such a very ragged and half-starved condition. The Indians were afraid they were going to be separated from us and would not leave us, and the Company thought they had better put up a tent for them in the lot where I lived. They would not go outside the fence for a week as they appeared afraid other Indians might kill them. At last we persuaded them to visit the Hudson's Bay store and the Company gave them as many blankets, muskets, etc. as their canoes could carry. The Company, fearing that some of the treacherous Cowichan tribe might attack and rob them, sent them on a small steamer with their canoes for some distance on their way home until they were out of danger of hostile Indians.

The Admiralty in London named a wide arm of the sea the "Homfray Channel", after me, not far from where the six Indians took us prisoners near Desolation Sound.

Many people in Victoria wished me to publish this account of our dangerous trip but I hesitated, as from my descriptions of the many dangers encountered Mr. Waddington was afraid that it would prevent parties joining him in making the road through to Cariboo.

*Two Homalco men and their canoe, twelve miles from
the mouth of the Homathko River, 1870s.*

CHAPTER 3

Yay K̲ Wum

I MET HERMAN FRANCIS painting his fish boat at the dock at Squirrel Cove. I asked him who the Klahoose chief might have been in 1861.

"What year did you say?"

"1861."

He smiled and went on painting the *Mona Lisa*.

"Down in Sliammon – they might know. There's some records."

In July at the Sliammon Seven-Aside Soccer Tournament, Calvin Harry said: "Talk to Keek̲us" – Liz Harry, a Klahoose elder – "she'll know."

On Sunday morning Keek̲us and I sat on her front porch in the sun.

"1861? – at the Brem?" she said. "You mean Kw'ikw'tichenaw – Salmon Bay?" Keek̲us worked back. "The last hereditary chief was Johnny Dominick – Hewk̲in. He was the informant for ethnographer Homer Barnett's book *The Coast Salish*. Hewk̲in died at 89 in 1954. His father was Yay K̲ Wum and that could have been Homfray's rescuer. People would have been smoking salmon at Salmon Bay that time of year."

It was a beautiful morning. Bells rang from the old church down by the water. "Lets talk to my sister Susan, she knows more than I do."

Liz's husband, Pete Harry, who is from the Homalco band native to

Bute Inlet, got out the van. As we drove to the soccer field I asked if they recalled any stories about the Chilcotin War. Liz turned to Pete:

"Was that when the Tsîlhqot'in came and killed some nineteen Homalco people in 1844?"

"No." Pete gently negotiated the entry onto the highway. "It was when they killed a group of men who were building a road up Bute Inlet. They came down into the Homathko valley and killed all the road crew, got captured and hung." He quickly glanced at me: "That story, it came down through my people, from a man who was there and survived; returned home to the village."

Suddenly we were at the field. Two games of soccer were going on at once. Other teams were warming up. Spectators lounged in the sun. Liz introduced me to her son, a grandchild, a niece, her sister Susan Pielle, Susan's daughter and her child. Susan (Thapwut), who is expert in her own language and teaches it to the children in the Sliammon school, spread a blanket. Pete placed a chair just behind to listen. When I asked Susan and Liz about Tsîlhqot'in coming down into their territory they said,

"Well they sometimes came to marry our girls."

When I asked why, they simultaneously patted their cheeks and laughed.

"We had these nice round cheeks."

They teased each other and me until I laughed so hard I couldn't ask any more questions. My husband's team got beaten by Calvin's. Calvin took off his canary-yellow Sliammon t-shirt and gave it to Bobo. The sun was hot, the trees tall and the shadows long.

What was now a contextualized series of events I had, up to this time, taken from the newspapers of the 1860s, books, reports, and letters in the archives. Some of the tales had seemed tall, but perhaps they were traps for culturally biased assumptions. History might just be stories one tells, revises and adjusts to audiences who are encouraged, in different eras, to wear differently coloured and patterned glasses through which to look back. As I had begun to assemble material around Homfray's journey, composer and film maker Trin T. Minh Ha, in a talk at the Museum of Anthropology at the University of British Columbia, spoke of a "journal re-formed to expose its original fiction" – "truths", she said – not "Truth".

Later, at Salmon Bay, I discovered a pictograph panel. Three human figures, one with a skirt, were dwarfed by a bird lifting a fish. It reminded me of what Valdes had written about the clever Straight of Juan de Fuca Chief Tetacus who he met in 1792:

"He took my notebook and pencil and drew a picture of a bird called Suayuk. He said that he had, with his own eyes, seen this bird lift a whale out of the sea. When I remonstrated with him that he must have been dreaming at the time he assured me he was as awake as I at this moment."

An eagle lifting a fish? A mythical creature? It could, of course, be a version of the Nentselgha7etsish that haunts the Homathko Canyon and drags your guts out by your backside. It could be a relative of the bird known in Kwak'wala as Hokhokw, splitter of skulls, eater of brains. These creatures, like the native place names, seem codes to culturally sanctioned states of mind, historical events, or guides to movement through and behaviour in, the landscape.

Speaking of the time when she had lived in Toba Inlet as a child, Susan said:

"At Kw'ikw'tichenaw, my mother told me, once, long ago, the Klahoose people saw a creature with huge white wings come into Toba Inlet. They were very afraid. All the women and children ran and hid up the river. Three men stayed to see what was coming and they heard a young man call out in their language from the creature. Amazed, they called back. Then a schooner came in with all kinds of people on it who gave our people many presents including flour and pilot biscuits in wooden boxes. They tried to eat the biscuits, but you know they're hard as wood, and they didn't know what to do with the flour. After a while they threw it in the river but it all floated out into the bay and eddied around the ship. My Mother said, 'If I had been there I would have been so embarrassed!' "

*'Village of the Friendly Indians', an engraving from George
Vancouver's* Voyage of Discovery, *shows a Homalco camp
at the mouth of Bute Inlet.*

CHAPTER 4

Up the Amazon
to Tibet

JULY 18, 1991 – Mixed cloud and sun, sea a slight ripple. Left Refuge at 8:30 and cruised straight up Lewis Channel stopping only for our good luck tin cup drink at the small waterfall opposite Bullock Bluff. Headed north, via Calm Channel, to look for Waddington's road and complete my tracing of Homfray's trip. We have no idea of the condition of the Homathko River but we only draw eight inches in our boat, the *Tetacus*. I've got three days' food, sleeping bags, inflatable mattresses, canned milk, juice in the cooler, dried soup.

We stop at U7p (Aupe), now Church House, to see if the Homalco band is still trying to raise salmon here. The church, built in 1896, is the oldest building in this area. A bust of Jesus leans out from the steeple toward Múushkin (Old Church House) across the channel. In 1890, the infamous Bute wind raced down the Inlet and flattened that village.

We cross the mouth of Bute Inlet toward "Angostura de los Comandantes," so named by the Spanish in 1792. It is one of the three sets of tidal rapids that constrict this route north. Now known as Arran Rapids, it can reach maximum velocities of nine knots with eight-foot overfalls. The duration of slack water is usually not more than five minutes.

Here, both the English and Spanish explorers met people who were at pains to help them traverse the whirlpools. Vancouver's journal contains an engraving of "The Village of the Friendly Indians." The Spanish narrative, translated in 1930 by Cecil Jane and published as *A Spanish Voyage to Vancouver and the Northwest Coast of America*, explains:

> [We] saw a large settlement situated in the pleasant plain on the west point of the mouth of the channel of Quintano [Bute Inlet] and proceeded to coast along to the mouth of Angostura. … In the neighbourhood there were a large number of canoes with two or three Indians in each, engaged in sardine [herring] fishing. … Many of the natives approached our officers without showing the least nervousness. These men were of medium height, well built, strong, of a darkish colour, and in their appearance, language, clothing and arms not different from those within the straight.

The people warned the Spanish against this passage, but when they persisted, they were informed at what angle of the sun they must go. At three o'clock the flood began to slacken and they attempted to row along a back eddy on the western shore. The 45-foot *Sutil* caught the ebb and was carried into mid-channel and then against the rocky shore. Out of control, she spun around three times until the sailors were dizzy. In the end, both the *Sutil* and the *Mexicana* reached another cove, possibly Vancouver Bay, the site of a village called Saaiyuck. The Spanish narrator claimed that this was the most terrifying event in their voyage.

The channel between Stuart Island and the mainland was named Arran Rapids by Vancouver after the Isle of Arran, home of the third Earl of Bute, a friend of the Royal family.* His continued patronage was sought by sprinkling his titles over bits of geography in this designative way. Little regard was given to the code of descriptive names developed by the native people.

We enter the inlet proper and at Amor Point, below Cosmos Heights, the water suddenly becomes an opaque jade path. The scale increases.

* The Earl of Bute's 16-year-old son, the Honorable Charles Stuart, served on board the *Discovery*'s sister ship the *Chatham*. He was implicated in the arrogant behaviour of Thomas Pitt, later Lord

Liquid light in a 1,000-foot freefall licks walls of steel. If we turn off the engine there are two sounds – a choral note of wind vibrating a billion fir needles, and a roar. Paradise River. Aurora Falls.

Past Clipper Point we head to the Orford River. Here at Pi7pknech ("white a little bit on the back end"), a Homalco winter village, we tie up to a piling and eat lunch. Two years ago, intoxicated by the intense green bay and the spicy smell of the river, we nosed the boat on and on through the hanging trees until we grounded on a sand bar. A vast valley struck northeast parting serious mountains. It was like going up the Amazon to Tibet. After that I thought of nothing but returning.

Bear Bay basin opens and a creek filters out. The canyon contracts again and a small sign of habitation appears below the Southgate River. Up, way up, a glacier burns like an opal. Turquoise pillars porch crystal caves. At the left of the river mouth a new stone stage has been blasted raw for a log sort, and a fresh boom hangs off stiff-legs "Scar Creek Logging."

We enter the Homathko at high slack. Scrubby low land on the right, miniature logging truck high on left. The driver waves, wondering. Cumsack River branches off left to the old Homalco village of Xwé-mallıkwu (Swift Water) that Pete Harry says was on stilts. An animal flicks and is gone. Silt banks collapse and flush downstream. As we pull away from the tide, the river broadens out. The current strengthens. It is like driving through mud.

The river suddenly bends sharp to the left, and sandbars almost block the way. On the right, a jumble of logs and, improbably, lights on poles. We manage to broach the eddies and whirlpools and attach ourselves to the fragile dock. The silence is fierce, mesmerising and total. Bobo goes to seek information. I hear voices, an arm waves me forward, and I see our old friend, Sam.

"Can ya stay a while? Hope ya didn't bring nothing to eat."

I follow him into the cookhouse trailer. He is here alone, camp-sitting, as he does all winter, but just now he is here for a week while the loggers go to town. Sam pours coffee from a ten-litre brewer. White arborite

Camelford, who was twice flogged by Vancouver in an attempt to maintain discipline. Vancouver's brother John claimed the public humiliation of an attack on Vancouver by Camelford in London (recorded in a contemporary cartoon as 'The Caning in Conduit Street') contributed, with the undiagnosed illness manifested at Teakerne Arm and the British government's delay in paying him his back wages, to his death at 41.

46　*High Slack*

tables, paper napkins neat in glasses, and around the walls on shelves, in coolers and fridges, is a bewildering array of food. There are quiches, pizzas, paté, cheese of many kinds, and cookies (peanut butter, chocolate chip). There are nanaimo and date bars, a dozen pies (pecan, apple, raisin and cherry), and Jello (red, yellow and green). There is juice of every known variety. Sam, gravely, takes Bobo to see the freezers, full to the tops with meat. He suggests a snack. I tentatively mouth a pink square of something, but it's like being offered an elephant for lunch. Where do you start?

We eat quiche, several slices of pizza, some pecan pie and cookies. Sam, thin as a dried bone, smokes. About our mission to find Waddington's road, he says, "Well, let's go for a drive. I'll gas up the boss's new four-wheel drive. The pickup is a pile of junk. It already broke down once last winter. Went up the road about twenty kilometres and I got a flat tire. Well, jeeze, I had to walk all the way and it was pretty cold and I had to pack the gun, ya know, because the wolves are everywhere in the winter, and so I walked back all the way down the river. My God, I was tired. Never been so tired in my life. Then, the next day, I get this truck and fill it up with gas and I drive it to the other truck, jack that up and change the tire. Then I drove the second truck a mile – walk back and drive the first truck to the second and so on and so on. Takes me another day. My God, I was worn out again. I'm 62, ya know."

Sam gasses up the half-ton and we head north out of the camp with his dog Rosco on my knee, the camp's black labrador in the box, and the river on the left. Soon, the road broadens out into a landing strip, which is how Sam and the loggers get here. It's the only place Waddington's road could have been. Upriver, we see two bears on the road. They stop, turn, take a good look and stroll off into the alder. As the valley opens out the lab makes a game of bounding out of the box and running just in front of the truck. We stop repeatedly to put him back in. This allows me to take the kind of photographs that later on, when we look at them, give no indication whatsoever of scale or glory.

We follow the valley for fifteen kilometers, see a deer and two fawns,

FACING PAGE: *View of Homathko River mouth, looking past Potato Point, Waddington Harbour, toward Bute Inlet.*

then veer right and start to rise. We cross an enormous log bridge over a shallow rage of gravelly water. The crossing is brand new, as is the dock our boat is tied to, the previous structures having been blown out last winter. Sam heads determinedly up and up and up, pausing for heart-stopping views of the river valley and the Coast Range. The road is merely a rock ledge blasted free of the matrix and bulldozed flat. It winds up tight as a belt against the mountainside.

Another bridge. I am filled with the sound of a torrent blasting from a miniature version of the canyon Waddington attempted to build a can-tilevered road through. The impossibility of the 1861 task is made plain when we pass the equipment needed now to build roads. The graders are two stories high.

The road deteriorates into roughly arranged boulders with bark filler. Sam persists. I clutch Roscoe. We reach the first-aid truck, a relic from World War II which I'm sure we will soon need. Suddenly we are in the open in front of an ice bridge. Here Sam and the road builder dug out a snow slide that buried the road last year.

"Now, I know you don't believe it was 47 feet deep," Sam says, "but it was because I crawled up on 'er with a tape and we measured."

Sam and Bobo stand in front of it and I back up out over the drop to get a wide-angle shot of the road, ice, the creek that has tunnelled through, and the almost vertical crack it slid from, and I am amazed to see they are dwarfed by an ice bridge still twenty feet high. The scale of everything is incomprehensible. We are like ants.

I amble around and let the guys go up and turn around. I can contemplate heights better with my feet on the ground. The truck is wonderful, but down is more terrifying than up, and the lab persists in bounding off and running just ahead of it. We have to stop, put him in the box, drive on. He forgets and jumps out again. We stop. It adds another kind of rhythm, another layer of apprehension. Sam pulls up at each 1,000-foot precipice. We gaze out at the cloud-scarved Wadding-ton ice field, stunned to be here and have free range of the place. I can't really speak, can only moan in ecstasy. I'm lucky to be with such taci-

turn men. No idle chatter, no "Ooh! Ah!" and no "How beautiful!"

Everywhere that has been logged is full of enormous sun-struck rasp-berries, better than any I have tasted. The air is full of birds. Swallows cut and arc like surveyors. Steller's jays screech. Beavers have dammed a sluggish pond way up high. New growth is rampant, but the clearcut-ting is formidable and the roads are brutal.

Back down along the river it's clear this road is often exactly where the old road was. There isn't any other place they could have put it. We stop

The Homathko River, in a 1865 watercolour by Frederick Whymper.

at remnants of a real homestead. Quite a few people tried to farm here from the time of the roadbuilding until 1900, but, as in Toba Inlet, the climate and isolation defeated them. At this point, there is a chaotic overlay of logging obliterating the Royal Engineer's careful grid for a town, and the spring floods alter the course of the river yearly.

Back at what I am convinced was to be the "Town of Waddington" we are presented with a period trailer from kitsch hell. An orange shag rug that should be put out of its misery, a purple sofa and grey plastic flowers, but we gratefully shower and test the bed. Bobo, drawn to the freezers like a bear to honey, finds giant steaks and we dine on the deck.

Sam says he likes the winters alone.

"Sure does get cold, though. Last winter, I came in first of December. One night, my second week, I went to sleep and it was two degrees. I keep a diary of temperatures and try to keep track. I hate to sleep with that generator banging next to my head so I turn it off at night. When I woke up it was 35 below, no kidding, and so I get up and try to start her and Jesus, I can't. No way. So I stay without lights for four days and it's cold as hell, but I got propane heat alright, so it's okay.

"Does the wind blow? Are you kidding? See that workshop down there, that big two-storey aluminum shed? It's for fixing the road building equipment. Well, last winter the wind really picked up and she blew all night and the temperature dropped to 32 degrees. In the morning those two twelve-foot doors, well, they were straight out horizontal on their hangers like a lab's ears in the wind. Well, jeeze. I thought I'd better tie them down, so I worked all morning getting the doors down with a winch and a truck. I tied them down and backed a half-ton up against them. Came out the next morning and they'd bellied out and pushed the truck four feet from the wall. It was a 'Bute', alright."

At nightfall, the valley is a luminous cobalt globe. A bear truffles at the edge of the camp until the lab puts it to rout. Sam's little dog sleeps. It's been a big day. As the moon rises, I prowl the shag, draw back the orange nylon lace curtains, shift the plastic blossoms on the vintage pink arborite table and watch its journey, too thrilled to miss a moment.

In *The Unknown Mountain*, held open to the pale light, I can just make out Don Munday's description of his first sight of what came, at his insistence, to be called Mount Waddington. In September of 1925 he and his wife Phyllis set out to prove that high, unclimbed peaks existed within the Coast Range. Unlike us, they were able to take the Union Steamship Company's *Chelohsin* from Vancouver as far as Orford River. En route, they were entertained with stories by the Reverend George Pringle of Texada Island, who had the honour to marry my mother to my father. Jack McPhee, a Bute trapper, ferried the Mundays to the base of Mount Rodney for a preliminary expedition.

> While pathfinding ahead of the party I pushed through thick brush to the brink of a windy precipice at a height of about 2,500 feet. Below me stretched the broad fiord, mightily walled; remnants of winter avalanches remained unmelted still in gullies within a few hundred feet of sea-level.
>
> Beyond – the scene is unforgettable – the 8,000-foot trench of the Homathko River extended north-west for about 20 miles from the head of Bute Inlet; a vast expanse of glacier seemingly closed the end of this great corridor, and out of the whiteness sprang a range of splendid rock towers. Wintry cloud roofed them. Piercing this in lonely majesty towered the nameless sovereign of an unknown realm.
>
> A climber has little quarrel with fate if he has been granted one such supreme moment. From this elevation, however, we could not well judge comparative heights of the mountains.

The next day, having gained the peak of Mount Rodney, he continues:

> The height becomes less insignificant – 7,843 feet – if it be recalled that this also represents direct uplift from Bute Inlet. Most of the neighbouring mountains were higher. Directly across the gorge of the Southgate River rose a summit of more than 9,000 feet, which we named Bute Mountain …

Of course the compelling interest of the panorama centred in the great range reared against the sky on the west side of the Homathko River. To us an aspect of unreality clung to it, for if some of the great peaks towered to 11,000 and 12,000 feet – and they looked all of that – then the great pinnacle exceeded 13,000 feet! But who would believe us?

At first light, the lab and I prowl the edges of the camp. Past a marooned ice cream truck, my foot locks midstep on what is a fragment, surely, of the 1862 road smothered in alder. I balance there, locked in a triangular gap between Waddington's ambitions, the Tsîlhqot'in resistance and implacable reclamation.

I come to, somehow, at the centre of the camp in what is a small white hospital. The clean, cool bed is surrounded by tall, white curtains. A green and red plaid blanket lies neatly folded on a crisp sheet. Red cross on a white enamel tin, tongue depressors in a glass jar, folded bandages. Foliage presses against the windows as it did, dog rose petals and leaves, against the surgery window at the Blubber Bay mine on Texada Island. Dr. Schwam, three-piece suit and watch chain across his "corporation," irritates my mother, who has run all the way from Gram's with me in her arms, by making her re-enter by the front door. My left index finger, sliced to the bone cutting carrots, he stitched to a semicircular white scar.

Bobo breaks in to announce breakfast. Bacon, eggs, ham, toast, jam – and quiche slathered with paté, if we so desire. "Coffee please," Sam says. He rolls a cigarette and tilts back a chair.

"Naw, I don't get many visitors. You're the second. Last winter we had a lot of snow. Been blowing hard for days. Got up one morning and it'd stopped, sun coming out. I was standing in the cook house sipping on my coffee. Looked up. There was a girl! Looking in the window. I couldn't believe it. Thought I was hallucinating. But there she was. A girl. She'd skied down from the glacier and all the way down that road out there toward the Teaquahan. Blew me away, it did. She and her boyfriend had been dumped on the glacier for a week's skiing by a helicopter, but they had three days of blizzards. They were pretty well stuck in a tent and ran out of food, so she skied down the road. Boy, was she hungry, but more than that she wanted a bath. Had to get on the radio phone and call in a plane."

He walks us back of the camp to the waterfall and along a flat, sweet road to the Teaqualian River which runs straight down, in a turquoise torrent, from the opaline glacier. The lab jumps into the icewater after sticks as I hold my breath. After lunch, the last cloud is gone and we jump in the truck and head back up the valley. Mount Waddington stands clear above its icy collar, implacable beyond the blooming fireweed. As we rise, each new turn and twist angles a new vista, each stop marks some ascension in wonder.

Back at camp, Bobo insists it's time to leave. Sam refills our gas tank because Stuart Island will be closed, and we set out, dragging my soul downstream.

JULY 23 – In my sketch book I write:

Purple Prose / Moon Rose (2 panels of silk).

The air from the glacier was like champagne, the river turquoise. We had stayed too long up the Homathko, and had to hurry down the inlet to make home before dark. The steep sides, drenched in rainbowed cascades by day, had become an iron tunnel.

As the channel bellied out between Bear Bay and Purcell Point, abrupt square waves formed at the meeting of the ebbing tide and the wind from the south. They sat up and held their form like jade lit from within. We became figures in a carving made from multi-coloured stone: ox-blood mountains, a luminous green sea, white jade for the boat.

"And what were you?"

Two figures frozen in an immense gem of time:

> *Every discoloration of the stone,*
> *Every accidental crack or dent,*
> *Seems a watercourse or an avalanche.*

"And what did you do there, frozen in time?"

Twisted and turned, unable to proceed, and went back up the swirling dark river – up the moon rose – to sleep again in the logger's camp, rise before dawn and cruise down the inlet with the sun. No jade waves rose and only as we turned at the Paradise River did the wind chop the sea dark and slow us down.

"Then?"

> *… the mountain … the sky …*
> *On all … the … scene they stare …*
> *Their eyes …*
> *Their ancient, glittering eyes, are gay.**

* From "Lapis Lazuli" by William Butler Yeats.

We were home before breakfast.

CHAPTER 5
Shadow

THE CHILCOTIN WAR, THE SHADOW to Homfray's and to my journey, is an event recorded from many points of view. Protagonists crawl out of drawers and folders, materialize foggily on machines, whisper: "I saw, with my own eyes, the … "

Native people tell a differently motivated but coeval story. "Shadow" is a search for pattern and form in the textual artifacts as found: not about the native story that is still to be written down, but beside it.

In the summer of 1993, the Nemiah Band of the Tsîlhqot'in nation (the Xeni qwet'in) demanded from the Province of British Columbia an official pardon for six Tsîlhqot'in men hanged in 1864 and 1865. During those years, the colonial authorities pursued, entrapped, and prosecuted these men for the murder of fourteen members of the Bute Inlet road crew and causing the death of seven other people. The Xeni qwet'in say that Tsîlhqot'in territory was never conquered because the people did not lose the deniduhl'zan – the war they declared on intruders in their land.

It might be said that both sides base their position on the assumption that war, like a game, has rules but murder does not. Few people, however, would admit that using Korean women as Japanese soldier "com-

JAMES DOUGLAS: *Born Demerara, British Guiana, 1803, son of John Douglas of Glasgow and a 'Creole' or 'Jamaican' woman. He entered the service of the Hudson's Bay Company in 1821 and married 'after the custom of the country' Amelia, the daughter of Chief Factor Connolly whose wife was a Cree 'princess'. In 1848, Douglas established Fort Camosun, which later became Victoria. He was*

fort," or the mass rape of enemy women, is "fair play" or "sporting". Only recently has rape been officially proposed as a war crime. Who gets to make these rules? Dozens of male participants in the events of 1864 can be named, but it is difficult to track the names and fates of the women involved. Nonetheless, both historical and contemporary native statements force one to attend to the claim that the sexual abuse of the daughter of a chief caused the war.

The history of these events is still embedded in an *embarras* of conflicting opinion, letters, dispatches, photographs and oral history. "Shadow" maps a rough route through these misunderstandings. But a map is not the territory, fragments restored are never a culture and, one hopes, not assumed to represent one. Like preliminary sketches for a portrait, they aim toward a likeness. Form and conjunction are inevitably seen from the position of the observer. Police Commisioner Chartres Brew writes to Governor Frederick Seymour in his clear firm hand on seductive blue-violet foolscap. I accept his criticism of Waddington and his statement that the misuse of women was part of the cause of the war.

Perhaps an operatic model can clear a path through the paper underbrush. Here is a cast of characters, and each has his/her part to sing which contributes to the whole. A weeping chorus of women laments on the side, there are fools, knaves, braves, a terrifying plague.

Shadow

OVERTURE

Father A. G. Morice, in *The History of the Northern Interior of British Columbia*, reports that in January 1849, Donald McLean, an officer of the Hudson's Bay Company in charge of Fort Chilcotin in the 1840s, headed a search party for native man named Tlhelh, who had allegedly killed a Company employee named Belanger. An eyewitness recounted:

"Arrived at the Quesnel Village, noticed that, tho this was deserted, 3 huts on the opposite side of the river seemed to be inhabited. Repairing thither, entered one, where found Tlhelh's uncle and his step-daughter and babe.

"McLean: 'Where is Tlhelh?'

" 'Tlhelh is not here,' Nadetnoerh replied.

" 'Where is he? Tell me quick,' insisted McLean.

" 'How can I know his whereabouts?'

" 'Then you shall be Tlhelh for today,' declared the white man, who, firing ... shot the Indian dead ...

"A son-in-law, in a hut cutting up venison, ran out ... [and] was dropped with several bullets from posse members. His half-breed wife attempted to hide in their hut, but one of the party went in and fired almost point-blank ... the ball crushed the baby's head and wounded the mother ...

"An old man blocked the entrance to the third hut and when McLean cut a hole in the roof and looked in, [McLean] almost blew his head off with a rifle shot.

"Months later, McLean got his man by threatening another uncle with the alternative of death for refusing to help, or 100 skins reward for Tlhelh's scalp. The uncle ... found his nephew and killed him, later whipping McLean's face with his scalp."

In March, 1850, Donald McLean wrote, regarding relations with native people, "hang first, then call a jury to find guilty or not-guilty."

ACT I

Scene I: Victoria, Vancouver's Island

APRIL 16, 1856 – Governor James Douglas to the Right Honourable Henry Labouchere:

"Sir: I hasten to communicate for the information of her Majesty's Government, a discovery of great importance, made known to me by Mr. Angus McDonald ... That gentlemen reports, in a letter dated on the 1st of March last, that gold has been found in considerable quantities within the British Territory, on the Upper Columbia."*

JULY 15, 1857 – "A new element of difficulty in exploring the gold

governor of the colonies of Vancouver Island and British Columbia, and retired as Sir James.

'Douglas was the most prominent man of the country, and the history of his life is very largely the history of British Columbia til 1865,' wrote John Walbran. 'For many years his authority as almost absolute ruler over the immense area which now constitutes BC was undisputed, and his fidelity to duty, his uprightness and impartial justice was known to Europeans and Indians alike.'

Amelia Douglas.

* From *Correspondence Relative to the Discovery of Gold.*

country has been interposed through the opposition of the native tribes of the Thompson's River who have lately taken the high handed, though not unwise course, of expelling all the parties of gold diggers, composed chiefly of persons from the American territories, who had forced entrance into their country. They have also openly expressed a determination to resist all attempts at working gold in any of the streams flowing into Thompson's River both from a desire to monopolise the precious metal for their own benefit, and from a well founded impression that the shoals of salmon which annually ascend these rivers ... will be driven off, and prevented from making their annual migrations."*

* *Ibid.*

AUGUST 2, 1858 – A Proclamation by Governor Douglas:

"British Columbia shall for the purposes of the Act be held to comprise all such territories Within the Dominions of Her Majesty as are bounded to the South by the Frontier of the United States of America, to the East by the main chain of the Rocky Mountains, to the North by Simpson's River and the Findley Branch of the Peace River, and to the West by the Pacific Ocean, and shall include Queen Charlotte's Islands and all other Islands adjacent to the said Territories, except as hereafter excepted."

Herman Francis Reinhardt, in *The Golden Frontier*:

"A miner told me he was in Victoria in June 1858 and at the height of the gold excitement for the Fraser River, and that there were over 10,000 miners in Victoria, and the Indians from up north in their large war canoes ... were trading with the Hudson's Bay Co. Stores, and the squaws got badly demoralised and the miners had plenty of money to spend with them, and they gave them whisky."

Scene II. Tsîlhqot'in Territory, Autumn 1861

From *Klatsassan and Other Reminiscences*, by the Reverend Lundin Brown:

"Fort Alexander is the chief post of the Hudson's Bay Company in that district. ... The agent received me with the hospitality which characterizes the Company's servants ... [and] told me of a tribe of Indians who were … encamped on a hill-side, not far from the fort. … I proceeded to speak to them the message of salvation. … One appeared more attentive than the rest. … His was a striking looking face; the great under-jaw betokened strong power of will; the eyes, which were not black, like most Indians, but of a very dark blue, and full of a strange, it might be dangerous light, were keen and searching. He never took them off the speaker but seemed to be perusing with them my innermost soul, as if

A woman panning for gold, 1860s.

LHA TSES'IN: *Various spellings (Klatsassan, Lhasas7in); principal war-chief of the Tsîlhqot'in. This engraving is from* Klatsassan, and Other Reminiscences of Missionary Life in British Columbia, *by the Reverend Robert Christopher Lundin Brown, about the uprising in 1864.*

he meant to ascertain not only whether I spoke true, but whether I believed in my heart what I said. When the service was over, this man came up to me, and without a word proceeded to fumble in my breast. I hardly relished this but I merely asked what he wanted. Upon this he pulled out of his bosom a crucifix which was tied round his neck. He said he wanted in fact to see whether I had what he had been taught to recognize as the mark of the true priest. …

"I had no crucifix, I was accordingly in danger of rejection as a false priest. I told him however, that I was a 'King George' or English Priest … and wore no crucifix … but carried it inside my heart. …

"His name was Klatsassan. He was a great man amongst the Indians … although not a hereditary chief-tan, he was looked upon as their chief by all the Chilcotins."

Scene III: Victoria

THE BRITISH COLONIST, MAY, 1861 – "FROM THE NORTH-WEST COAST AND BUTE INLET: Mr. Herman Shipper … arrived yesterday on the schooner *Nonpareil* from a trading voyage … on the 28th of April the *Nonpareil* entered Bute Inlet and ascended to its head. They found the country very inviting in its appearance and during their stay 5 feet of snow fell. The mountains are high and in many cases descend to the water's edge. The tide in ebbing and flowing in the inlet runs at the rate of 8-10 knots and navigation is rendered not only disagreeable but it is also at times unsafe from a chop sea which continually prevails. At the head of the inlet is quite a large flat, in front of which good anchorage and shelter from the winds are to be had. This flat has been staked by the Hudson's Bay Co. … in anticipation of the founding of the town there. Near the entrance to the inlet are a few Indian huts and at its head there are also a few lodges. With regard to a route to the interior Mr. Shipper says he found one Indian … who told him the Buteites could travel and often did so – from the coast to Alexandria and back in 14 days. The route … was over precipitous mountains on the sides of which it was extremely difficult to maintain a footing. Once over

WADDINGTON!

Great Sale of Town Lots!!

Rousing Opportunity!!!

On the 1st of April, will be offered, on the ground, 5,000 Town Lots, being the entire site of WADDINGTON, at the head of Dean's Channel, on the North Coast of British Columbia.

A few citizens of Victoria, having been moved by a philanthropic desire to build up a Town at that point, are prepared to offer *Extraordinary Inducements*! And, in order that said point may be the seaport of British Columbia, steps will be taken to fill up the present "dangerous" entrance to Fraser River and Burrard Inlet.

For plans, and further particulars, apply at the Waddington Office, #10 Siwash Alley, Victoria.

P.S. Should parties making purchases at the above sale desire to have half the purchase money refunded, the thing can be done, as the philanthropic citizens aforesaid have a way of managing such matters with the government. As the navigation is very bad at present, balloons will be provided to convey intending purchasers to the place of sale, free of charge.*

the mountains, the country was level. While Mr. Shipper was at the head of the inlet, an Indian endeavouring to ascend one of the mountains missed his footing and was dashed to pieces.

DECEMBER 21 – "We briefly noticed yesterday the return of Mr. Homfray and six others who left here two months since to survey the route from the head of Bute Inlet to the interior. It appears that the party had to endure the greatest suffering and privation on their return and that their lives were in jeopardy for more than a fortnight, owing to the loss of their canoe with nearly everything it contained … Finally when reduced to their last meal, they were rescued from what seemed certain death by the Indians of Desolation Sound. These Indians Mr. Waddington had made the acquaintance of … and on learning that the party had been sent by the 'old ty-hee from Victoria' … showed them every kindness, took the party to their lodges in Desolation Sound, fed and kept them, and finally brought them home to Victoria.

"With respect to the object for which the party was organized, the information is satisfactory. Price River [Homathko] is found to be navigable for forty miles with light draught steamboats and boats and canoes

* This editorial, written by John Robson, a future premier of the province, is from the New Westminster *British Columbian* of April 16, 1861.

Tsimshian smallpox mask of carved alder, with a mobile lower beak. The raised bumps are wooden pegs, inserted into the mask and painted red.

can ascend twelve miles higher at which point an easy portage is required to avoid a canyon, of about 350 yards in length."

MARCH 12, 1862 – "Following upon the first gold excitement of 1858, it became the habit of many of the northern coastal tribes to visit Victoria in large numbers, and at times more than 2,000 'Hydahs', 'Stickeens', 'Chimseans', 'Bella Bellas' and 'Fort Ruperts' were camped in the vicinity.

MARCH 18 – "There are reports that one case of varioloid [smallpox] exists in the town. The patient came from San Francisco, where the disease is prevalent, on the last steamer *en route* to the gold fields. The case is not considered dangerous by the attending physician. As our city is now however in almost weekly communication with the Bay city and, as miners and entrepreneurs head north, it is to be hoped that the citizens of this town and those heading for the mines will avail themselves of a vaccination.

"The patient identified is rooming in a thickly populated neighbourhood."

MARCH 28 – "The propriety of the establishment of a small-pox hospital is being urged by many citizens who dread that the disease may become prevalent in the colony in consequence of the susceptibility to contagion of Indians."

MARCH 29 – "BUTE INLET: The agreement to construct a mule trail from the head of Bute Inlet to the Fraser, was signed yesterday between Col. Moody and the grantee, Alfred Waddington, Esq. The trail is to be completed within 12 months. The toll to be levied is one cent and a half per pound of goods; one dollar per head on beef cattle and pack-animals, and fifty cents per head on sheep, goats and swine. The charter to be for five years from the date of the completion of the road."

APRIL 26 – "THE SMALL-POX AND THE INDIANS: On Thursday several Nettinet Indians called on the Governor and said that they had been deputized by their tribe to ascertain whether there was any truth in a story told them by some white scamps that Gov. Douglas was

Hannah Maynard's washer-woman, 1862.

about to send the small-pox among them for the purpose of killing off the tribe and getting their land. They were assured that they had been hoaxed."

APRIL 28 – "THE SMALL-POX AMONG THE INDIANS [Editorial]: When it was first intimated that one or two cases of varioloid had made the appearance in this place, we predicted that if proper preventions were not taken at once to prevent that loathesome disease from .spreading, the Indians on the Reserve would become infected and through them spread itself throughout the colony ... Were it likely that the disease would only spread among the Indians, there might be those among us, like our authorities, who would rest undisturbed, content that the small-pox is a fit successor to the moral ulcer that has festered at our doors through-out the last four years ...

"The Indians have free access to the town day and night. They line our streets, fill the pit of our theatre, are found at nearly every open door during the day and evening; and are even employed as servants.

"It requires no further comment to show what a terrible scourge we are nursing at our doors – a scourge that may strike down our best citizens at any moment ... What is more, the reports of such a disease existing among the Indians, is calculated to alarm immigrants."

MAY 7 – "The 'original' party who have been working on the Bute Road have returned. They completed a mile of the trail and built ten bridges and two store houses.

"The Euclataws were at first troublesome but finally allowed the party to work on being promised presents from 'Victoria Tyee' (Mr. Waddington). These Indians filled 20 canoes and were fishing for oolachans.

"Six Chilcotin Indians – three from the rapids above the canyon – and three direct from Alexandria, learning that there were whites came down to trade, but on seeing the Euclataws retreated and could not be prevailed upon to return. The river was rising on Wednesday last when the party left."

MAY 8 – "SMALL-POX AMONG THE INDIANS: We call particular attention of the authorities ... to the spread of the small-pox of the most virulent type among the Indians.

"The Chimseans were the first afflicted. There are now ten cases among them at the small-pox hospital erected by Rev. Mr. Garrett. Three Fort Ruperts died yesterday. The Rev. Mr. Garrett, after considerable difficulty, found seven cases among the Hydahs ... Gov. Douglas donated $100 yesterday to relieve the Indians. But what trifling it is with the lives of our own citizens to think private benevolence can afford the security for the public health that is demanded! We hope that before this paper is dry ... steps will be taken by the clergy and the fathers of families to protect the town by banishing the Indians, and provide something like Christian assistance to the poor wretches."

MAY 12 – "THE INDIANS: An effort will be made by the police to remove the Hydahs and Fort Ruperts from the Reserve today. Two of the Hydahs died yesterday ... The Chimseans and the Stickeens are encamped on small islands in the Canal de Haro, and the Songishes have taken possession of Discovery Island. Not one member of the latter tribe has yet been attacked with the disease."

MAY 14 – "THE SMALL-POX: Indian Huts on the Reserve were fired by order of the Police Commissioner and burned to the ground. The Indians were notified to leave on Saturday last, and three days having elapsed and no notice being taken of the warning, fire was resorted to for the purpose of compelling them to evacuate which they prepared to do yesterday after their houses had been levelled to the ground."

MAY 29 – "HOW TO GET RID OF A TROUBLESOME QUESTION [Editorial]: The order from the Police Superintendent requiring all Indian men and women to leave the town and vicinity instanter, not only affects those who may reside with partners of their own race, but also reaches many citizens who have co-habited with native women for years, and by whom they have children, without having the union legalized by marriage. This class of citizens is in a quandary. Their women have been warned off, and the men ... cannot accompany them, nor can they permit their offspring to do so, and thereby expose them to the small-pox and kindred diseases ... The women, with true motherly affection for their young, naturally refuse to be separated from them and threaten, if sent away, to skulk in the adjacent forest and steal the chil-

King Freezy, the Songhees chief who saved his people by taking them to Discovery Island.

A Tsîlhqot'in family.

dren at the first convenient opportunity ... the best plan that can be adopted is to make the best of a bad bargain and honest women of their paramours."

JUNE 6 – "SAD SCENES AT OGDEN POINT: Yesterday morning, Superintendent Smith, with Officer Weihe, started for Ogden Point for the purpose of ordering the Hydah Indians supposed to be encamped in that neighbourhood to leave for the North, and on nearing the Point were surprised to find a death-like stillness reigning over the neighbourhood and a strong smell of decaying animal matter pervading the atmosphere. The officers approached the spot cautiously and ascertained that several dead bodies were lying around corrupting and tainting the air with their foul exudations; and that out of 100 Indians who were encamped there two weeks ago, not one could be found. The houses were left open, as if the late occupants had stepped out intending to return in a few moments. Guns, pistols, knives, tools, dresses and trinkets lay scattered confusedly on the floors of the lodges. Here was to be seen a child's toy, there a gaudy-hued shawl or an elegant silk mantilla – and occasionally, a book or a daguerreotype was picked up. Everything seemed as if the intention of the owners was to return in a few moments, and so the officers remained in the vicinity for some time awaiting the appearance of some of the tribe. But they waited in vain, for they were soon informed by an Indian belonging to another tribe, that after all but 10 or 12 of the Hydahs had fallen victim to the ravages of the disease, the survivors on last Wednesday morning procured a canoe and started for the North, humanely taking their sick with them."

JUNE 14 – "Capt. Shaff of the Schooner *Nonpareil*, informs us that the Indians recently sent North from here are dying fast. As soon as pustules appear upon an occupant of one of the canoes, he is put ashore; a small piece of muslin, to serve as a tent, is raised over him, a small allowance of bread, fish, and water doled out and he is left alone to die. What were our philanthropists about that they were not up the coast ahead of the disease two months ago, engaged in vaccinating the poor wretches who have since fallen victims?"

THE TSÎLHQOT'IN PEOPLE: *Athapascan-speaking people of the Chilcotin Plateau. Their name also appears as 'Tsilh-qox-t'in' or 'Tsilhqox Dene'. 'Dene' or 't'ine' means 'person' or 'people'. 'Qox' or 'yeqox' means 'river'.*

Scene IV: Tsîlhqot'in Territory, 1862

Francis Poole, in *Queen Charlotte Islands: A Narrative of Discovery and Adventure in the North Pacific*, writes that while on a mining exploration inland from Bentinck Arm, two of the surveyors he had been with were taken sick with smallpox and had been left in the care of the Tsîlhqot'in Chief Annahim at Nancootlem.

ANNAHIM: *Tsîlhqot'in chief of the Nancootlem territory.*

LIEUT. HENRY S. PALMER, RE: *In 1862, while surveying in the Chilcotin country, got into trouble with Annahim's son Nawuntl'oo. He threatened to introduce a disease that would kill everyone.*

The journalist James Young, in a letter to a friend, October 20, 1862, describes his journey along the route of Lieut. Henry S. Palmer's trail, from Alexandria, on the Fraser River, to Bella Coola:

"Although I had been told by the packer McLeod of the devastation of the Chilcotin Indian village at Nancoolten I was unprepared for the reality.

"One afternoon we were skirting the edge of a lake, on the other side rose a wall of glorious snow-clad mountains when a nauseating smell assailed our nostrils. A breeze swept the smell away but it returned. Puzzled, we walked along the trail, and came upon a large Indian village of some 20-30 houses. No dogs appeared to warn the occupants.

"We are approaching a village of the dead, said Mr. Fortune. Look, and he pointed at two heaps of earth that looked much like a grave. More demonstrative was a heap of brush piled over another Indian corpse and beside this yet another partially wrapped in a blanket, when I saw flies crawling over the sightless eyes and decaying bodies I almost retched. Speechless, we realized this was Nancoolten.

"At the north end of the lake the smell of wood-smoke caught our attention, and by a stream a man sat by a fire in front of a brush hut. He was horribly pock marked but there was no fever on him. He had survived the tragic epidemic.

"When he saw us he rose to his feet. He had a knife in his hand from the look of anger and hatred on his face I wondered if he would attack the four of us.

" 'Cultus white man,' he shouted – 'Cultus white man bring small pox – kill all my people.'

"We tried to talk to him but without avail. Finally Mr. Fortune left some food for him and we hurried away not desiring an arrow in the back. But the Indian was too busy with the food to use an arrow. It is estimated that of the original 1,500 Chilcotin less than 1/2 survived."

Poole's narrative goes on to describe how Jim Taylor, a trader three miles up the Bella Coola valley, and another trader, named Angus MacLeod, decided to go up to Nancoolten. Since the Indians had ceased to bury their dead, and left them in the woods, the traders gathered up the blankets from the corpses and sold them to the surviving Tsîlhqot'in.

Poole maintained that the infected blankets started a new outbreak of smallpox, and McLeod himself died of the disease.

Scene V. Bute Inlet, 1863

Captain Frederick Saunders, in "Homatcho, or the Story of the Bute Inlet Expedition," relates that a 91 man party of Waddington's road-builders left Victoria for Bute Inlet in April, 1863, on the steamer *Enterprise.*

"The Homatchos with their chief (Nunimimum) were the first to greet our coming. This tribe of Indians is not large, but are free-hearted people, and particularly friendly to whites. Along with them were some of the Clayhoose tribe, who have intermarried with the Homatchos …

"The men were divided into sectional camps at about equal distances; the choppers and bridgers pioneering the course laid out by the surveyor through the valley, in close proximity to the river for about fifteen miles. The lines of the townsite were defined, and a wharf, with storehouse erected in that calm and beautiful sheet of water named Waddington Harbour. A few log houses were put up – two by the settlers accompanying us … and one large enough for the commissariat supplies, as headquarters, superintended by a Mr. Brewster.

"The first acquaintance with the Chilcoaten Indians was made here: there were only a few, as the main tribe rarely came so near the coast … from what one could discern there appeared a very marked difference in

THE HOMALCO PEOPLE:
A branch of the Coast Salish, a broad linguistic and cultural family that includes the Sliammon, Kluhoose and Island Comox. Main villages were on the Homathko and Southgate rivers and at Orford Bay in Bute Inlet. The pit houses on the west site of the Homathko have been identified as Homalco. The Tsîlhqot'in came down into the canyon in August to fish for coho. Sometimes the pass froze early and they were forced to winter in the canyo, and they would occupy these dwellings.

ALFRED PENDRELL WADDINGTON: *Born 1801, England. Educated in France and Germany. Grocer and entrepreneur, he arrived in Victoria in 1858. That year he wrote* The Fraser River Mines Vindicated, *the first book published in the Vancouver Island Colony. Served two terms as a member of the Vancouver Island assembly. In 1862 he helped draft Victoria's charter, and was superintendent of schools, 1865-66 The Canadian government bought his surveys for a cross-Canada rail route terminating at Bute Inlet.*

these Indians, to those previously met with: their clothing was decidedly scant; their features were haggard, describing almost a hungry look. Some wore rings in their noses, and their faces frightfully bedaubed with paint: the youngest men tying up the hair in a brush-like fashion at the side of the head …

"By the middle of June the road was completed satisfactorily up to the place where the crossing of the river came, a distance of about fifteen miles from the townsite …

"It was now the month of August, and the Chilcoaten Indians were expected about this time, as it is their usual custom to catch salmon on a creek nearby Canyon Camp; called Salmon Creek. The Clayhoose and Euclataw Indians claim their just rights on the valley of the Homatcho up to the head of the valley on the place called Salmon Ranch. The next tribe, a very small one, claim from thence to about a mile beyond the great canyon. They are a branch of Chilcoaten. The Chilcoaten tribe proper extends from the above point [northward]."

In a letter to the secretary of the Bute Inlet Company written May 23, 1863, Alfred Waddington describes the scene upon his arrival that spring at the Homathko River:

"We were not a little surprised on reaching here to find a long row of wooden huts built by the Indians along the front of the river in evident expectation of our arrival ... we had never seen a living Indian here before. They numbered from 200-250, composed of Clahoosh, Comox, Nicletaws and Chilcoaten Indians, all waiting their prey like vultures, and were not a little disappointed when they saw the mules landed and learned that these were to carry all the provisions. ...

"[A] small plunger was seen at the head of the inlet and the next day a number of our Indians were raving mad with drink."

REVEREND LUNDIN BROWN —"In the autumn [of 1863], a party who had gone to the Bute Inlet to survey for the new road, left there on their departure some 25 sacks of flour in a log house in the charge of an Indian named Chessus, one of the Chilcotin tribe. Chessus, however appears to have left the neighbourhood, and, during his absence, another tribe passing that way, had broken into the log-house and stolen the flour. When in the spring of 1864 our people returned to Bute Inlet, finding their flour gone, and no Indian near the place, they naturally caused inquiry to be made far and near. At last they got hold of some Chilcotin Indians, and asked them what had become of the flour .... At length one of them said, 'You are in our country; you owe us bread.'

"On this the man in charge ... began to take down, from the mouth of the interpreter the names of all the Indians present. When he asked if they knew what he had done, they said: 'No.' 'I have taken down your names,' he told them, 'because you would not tell who stole the flour.'

Frederick Whymper's water-colour of the upper entrance to the defile at the head of Bute Inlet. Waddington's road is on the right.

At this the Indians looked frightened, and he went on: 'All the Chilcotins are going to die. We shall send sickness into the country, which will kill them all.'

"So when those Chilcotins saw their names taken down and they heard themselves threatened with disease ... they recollected that something of the same sort had been said by another white man two years before, at a place called Puntzeen, in the interior; he had said smallpox was coming, and in the winter of 1862-63 it had come …

"It was not long before the news of this threat reached the ears of Klatsassan."

ACT II

Scene I. Bute Inlet

APRIL 18, 1864 – Artist Frederick Whymper, in search of "sublime" views to advertise Waddington's road, heads upriver.

"The route lay through a magnificent forest of cedar, hemlock, and Douglas pine, individual specimens of which almost rivalled the 'big trees' of California. One of the cedars measured forty-five feet in circumference at the butt.

"The road followed more or less the river valley, the scenery of which was not seen to advantage till, after crossing the stream by a rope-ferry, we commenced the ascent of a mountain by zigzag trail, in order to avoid the passage of a rock-grit canyon. From this the views were superb. Purple cliffs rose – pine-clad and abrupt – whilst below the Homathco made its way to the sea …

"On the 19th April, having arrived at the furthest camp of the constructing party … and, having secured the services of an Indian of some intelligence – Tellot by name – an old chief, I again started …

"Few can have any conception of the old forests through which our course lay, who have not themselves seen such. Now an immense fallen trunk, over which we had to climb, blocked the path; now one under which we were obliged to creep; and now and again, an accumulation of the same, the effect of some wintry storm or natural death. Here, as the tree falls so it lies, and has lain undisturbed for ages. …

"[A]fter following the Homathco River more or less closely for the greater part of a day, we reached the first glacier stream, and soon obtained a distant view of the great 'frozen torrent' itself, with the grand snow-peaks behind it …

FREDERICK WHYMPER: *An English artist hired by Waddington to make drawings to attract British investors. In 1868 he published* Travels and Adventures in the Territory of Alaska.

Inspector Chartres Brew

* Whymper, *Travels and Adventures in the Territory of Alaska.*

"We pitched our camp in an open space from which the snow had melted, on the flat of land extending for several miles below the glacier. On the next morning (24th April) after our simple repast, and one pipe, I left Tellot in camp and struggled up by myself to the base of the glacier, a distance of about two and a half miles, through very deep, but rotten and thawing snow. ...

"At its termination the glacier must have been three-quarters of a mile in width; it was considerably wider higher up. Whilst sketching it, all around was so supremely tranquil, that its action was very noticeable. Rocks and boulders fell from it sufficient to crush any too eager observer."

APRIL 28 – Having obtained his "views", Whymper heads down to the head of the inlet.

"I reached the station late in the evening and was soon fast asleep. Early the next morning, some friendly Indians broke into the room without warning and awoke us, saying in a excited and disjointed manner, that the man in charge of the Ferry had been murdered by the Chilcotins for refusing provisions in his care. We simply laughed at the idea ...

"The superintendent, Brewster, had entrusted letters of importance to me and had in fact rather hurried my departure. I therefore on the 30th of April left the river by canoe."*

Scene II. On the Bute Inlet Road

THE VICTORIA DAILY CHRONICLE, MAY 11 – "HORRIBLE MASSACRE: The steamer *Emily Harris* arrived from Nanaimo this morning. She brings three men as passengers who are the sole survivors of Waddington's party of seventeen workmen, the remaining fourteen having been massacred by Chilcotin Indians who had been hired to pack for them."

MAY 19 – Inspector Chartres Brew, police magistrate, acting as coroner, arrives at Bute Inlet and, guided by the Homalco Qwhittie, inspects the sites where the killings occurred. His report was gathered with other material into two typescripts in the BC Archives, called "Origins of the Massacre" and "A Survivor's Account".

"First Camp:

"The scene of desolation here was distressing beyond expression. All the tents had been cut up and were gone, and the whole camp gutted; or what was left, was smashed and destroyed – baking pans broken to pieces, cross-saws bent in two, books and papers torn up and scattered to the wind, with torn clothes and blood besmeared in every direction, but no bodies. It was easy, however, to trace them and find how each had been dragged to the river, by the blood on the stumps and the marks on the ground.

MAY 20 – "1st Tent – At the place where Oppenshaw's head lay, there was a large pool of blood. His hat was found close by. There was a pool of blood near the head of John Nieuman, who was next found. His shirt and trowsers were found, the first with two bullet holes near the right groin, the trowsers untouched. He had evidently been shot in bed when undressed, and probably finished with a blow on the head.

"2nd Tent – Blacksmith Scotty, a large pool of blood near the head. George Smith found in the same manner.

"3rd Tent – Robert Pollack, blankets saturated with blood; the inside of the straw matting all stained with blood; probably shot or wounded in the body. P. Peterson escaped wounded.

"4th Tent – Peter Buckley, escaped badly wounded. Hoffman, black jumper saturated with blood; white blanket the same; black necktie covered with blood, hair and brains; towel full of blood. There seems to have been a struggle for life. An empty leather purse found here covered with blood, and a canvas bag for silver.

"5th Tent – Charles Buttle, cook; no blood, the ground of the tent clean and smooth; his dark coloured jacket found near the fireplace with two bullet holes in the back; was evidently dressed and had just left the tent; was probably shot in the back while stooping over the fire; is supposed to have been shot the first.

"6th Tent – Joseph Fielding. His trowsers, which he was in the habit

QWHITTIE: *A Homalco man also known as 'Little George' or 'Tennas George'.*

of putting under his head, steeped in blood. James Campbell, straw matting full of blood, blue bed cover, the same. A remnant of the tent stabbed through. E. Mosely. He was in this tent and escaped unhurt; he had changed tent the evening before, unknown to the Indians.

"Third or Upper Camp:

"About two miles above the preceding. The ground was covered with debris as at the other camp and strewn with torn papers. It was near this spot, that P. Buckley, one of the wounded men, watched the Indians dividing the spoil in the evening; he was hid in a hole amongst the rocks above …

"The first body found was that of James Gaudet, lying against a tree on the hill-side, about 50 yards below the trail. A bullet had passed through the shoulder and a second through the left temple, the brain protruding through the wound. The body was naked except the socks, and in a shocking state of decomposition.

"The body of John Clark, the settler, found about 100 yards further on, and 75 yards from the trail, down the hillside. Bullet shot in the groin, another inside the right thigh, and the head battered. Body stripped and in a hideous state.

"Baptiste Demerest, the third in order, had evidently been chopping a few yards further on; must have seen or heard the first two shot; left the log he was at and ran for his life down the hill, after stopping under a tree where his handkerchief was found and recognized. His heel steps clearly traced down the hill to a mossy ground near the river, into which he either jumped of his own accord (for he was rather weak-minded) or was driven, and was dashed to pieces; or possibly he was taken prisoner, and may be still alive, for he spoke broken Chilcoaten, served as an interpreter, and was looked upon as a sort of 'Tilicum' by the Indians.

"The body of Mr. Brewster, the foreman of the party, was found about 200 yards further down the hill and near the last tree he had blazed. There was a bullet hole, in the right breast and the right temple was traversed by the sharp edge of an axe, which had penetrated to the brain. A large incision in the side showed that the body was empty and that the heart had been removed – to be cut up, probably and ate, as the greatest mark of Indian vengeance!! The body was naked, a woman's shoe, and Mr. Brewster's pocket and time books, and several letters from Mr. Waddington, were found near the body.

"A receipt from the Bank of British North America for $200 and two $20 bank-notes, belonging to P. Peterson, also, a receipt for $350 from the Bank of British Columbia, belonging to J. Campbell, were found amongst the stray papers. Peterson had also some coin; Clark had $230, and Joseph Fielding $50. Hoffman and some of the other men had money, all of which was plundered.

"Motives for the Massacre:

"Plunder was certainly one of the chief incentives; there can be little doubt, however, that the main object in view was to put a stop to a road through the Chilcoaten territory.

"The murder on the Bute Inlet Trail is but the continuation on a larger scale of those committed at Bella Coola, which have remained unpunished, and which prove the aversion of the Chilcoatens to the opening up of their country by the whites. The Bute Trail had lately entered on their territory, and no compensation had been offered them. Nor could Mr. Waddington, who had paid $2,000 of taxes on the road, be expected to do anything. Two years ago he succeeded in pacifying the small tribe below with presents, but when he applied to the Government for reimbursement, was told that he had done it on his own responsibility. As before stated, most of the Chilcoatens who committed the murder had come down to the trail for the first time, and Mr. Brewster and the workmen were particularly struck with this. There can be no doubt that these men decided the lower Chilcoatens to commit the deed, and that their intention was to include Mr. Waddington, as being the great tyhee and sole promoter of the enterprise … It is true that Mr. Brewster was less generous in giving them provisions than formerly … But though starving the Indians would never take food in payment for work … The upper Chilcoatens only hated Mr. Brewster inasmuch as they hated the whole enterprise … The mutilation of Brewster's body

BAPTISTE DEMEREST:
A Bute Inlet homesteader and a member of Brewster's road crew. Escaped the massacre, or was let go. Seems to have been the man who translated at the trial for Begbie and later for Lundin Brown, and thus would have witnessed the entire series of events.

was a well known act of warlike vengeance and the natural consequence of being at the head of the enterprise in Mr. Waddington's absence.

"A third and last conjecture may be given, which is the removal of Governor Douglas, whom the Indians had known for 30 years and for whom they had a profound respect. Nor can the Indians understand how a chief or Governor can be removed except by death.

"The Chilcoaten Indians who committed the crime were chiefly new faces, who had come down in the early spring this year, and were seen at the head of the inlet for the first time. The intention of Klattasen, the most influential amongst them, and the chief instigator, had been, however, to return to Benchee Lake by the Memeya and Bridge Rivers; he was only waiting, as he said, for Mr. Waddington's arrival, after whom he inquired anxiously every day, and whether he would bring many men and provisions with him. He said he wanted him to get back his daughter for him from the Euclataws. In the meantime his eldest boy Pierre, a lad of fifteen, went up with the packers on Wednesday, April 20th, to the Ferry where he had a long talk with the Chilcoatens, of the upper camp, and returned in the morning of Friday the 23rd, when his father Klattasen immediately changed his mind … He would now give a canoe, six blankets, and two muskets, for his daughter, and started on Tuesday morning, April the 26th, for the Ferry, with his young Indians, his two sons and daughters, and three squaws, slept at the halfway house or Slough camp, slept again near Boulder Creek, and reached the Ferry on Thursday morning, about 9 a.m. He probably murdered Smith, the Ferryman, the same evening.

"There were about two tons of provisions at the Ferry, all of which were removed, the skiff chopped to pieces, and the scow cast adrift. All this was done before 10 on Friday morning, for the murderers were met about 11 by the Clayoosh Indian, Squinteye, a mile higher up on the other side of the Ferry."

The BC Archives typescript includes a "declaration" by Squinteye. "He [Squinteye] was coming down to the Ferry from the upper camp on Thursday morning, with the chief Tellot, to fetch up provisions, when they met Klattasen," who said Squinteye and Tellot "need not go to the ferry, that they would find nobody there, for he had killed Smith. Tellot got angry, expostulated with Klattasen, and said he would return and inform Mr. Brewster, the foreman, but finally accompanied Klattasen, [who] then snatched away Squinteye's gun, giving him, or promising to give him, two blankets (a very small equivalent), and threatening otherwise to stab him. Klattasen then told Squinteye to be gone, as quick as he could down the valley, and say nothing, or he would be murdered also. Klattasen had on Smith's shirt with red stripes. They were going up the hill at the canyon about a mile above the Ferry, when he met them. This was about 11 a.m. Klattasen said that he would see the white men murdered because they did not give them their grub for packing."

APRIL 29 – "[Klattasen] proceeded it appears to join the other Indians at the principal camp about seven miles up, where they talked and joked with the workmen after supper, and sang Indian songs during a part of the night. The massacre took place just before the time the men generally arose in the morning and so simultaneously, that it is a wonder that anyone escaped to tell the tidings."

Qwhittie, who served as Brew's guide, testified at the subsequent trial of the six Chilcotins charged with murdering the road crew. The following is from the trial notes of Matthew Baillie Begbie. The parenthetical comments are Begbie's ("MBB").

APRIL 30 – "I was Brewster's cook. I had risen in the morning – made tea for the 4 men – After breakfasting 3 men went to work with axes – Brewster went ahead to mark the way – (blaze the line) – he said he would be back at noon. – I was washing up the plates when some Indians came up – 6 in all – 4 with muskets 2 without muskets. One of the 6 (a slave) said the white men would all be killed and I also. I said why will you kill me? He replied I don't know – go home to your own country – The Indians came from down the river. Chessus (the prisoner) is the only one of those 6 Indians who is now present. I then ran away down the trail.

"I met all the other prisoners coming up the trail. I saw that camp on my way down – there were 4 dead bodies in it – 2 in one tent, one in each of the 2 other tents. I knew Jim Clark … (witness meant Jim, *i.e.* James Gaudet – French Canadian and Clark *i.e.* John Clark both of whom it appeared subsequently were in Brewster's camp and murdered there – inquest held on them by Mr. Brew – MBB) Before I ran from Brewster's camp, I heard some shots – not far off – saw Jim running limping down the hill – I then ran away. Chessus had a gun when I saw him come up to Brewster's camp. The bodies at the lower camp were new killed but cold – knew the whole of the prisoners before – they had lived all last winter in my country. When I came to the ferry I found 2 white men there."

Reverend Dr. Grant accompanied Brew's expedition. He reported: "[A]mongst the articles scattered around the melancholy spot were at least one pair of women's boots – too surely indicating the source of the trouble."*

* Grant, *Ocean to Ocean*.

Scene III. The Chilcotin Plateau

Nancy, theTsîlhqot'in country wife of William Manning, gave the following sworn testimony, through interpreters, in the case of *Regina v. Tahpit*, regarding the murder of Manning at his homestead following the events on the Homathko River. The following is from Begbie's trial notes.

"I know Manning. I will tell the same story over again. Manning was working outside the house. Two Indian women came & told me the Indians were coming to kill him & advised me to leave for fear of being hurt. Manning asked why the 2 women were speaking. I told him they said the Indians had killed all the whites at Homalco and would come & kill him.

"He said, 'I don't believe the Chilcotins will hurt me. I have known them long, they like me & will give me the land.'

"I said, 'These are not Chilcotins, but from a distance. I don't know them. I am afraid & wish to go.'

"We went into the house & had dinner. Afterwards, Manning went out. An old woman came & said, 'Perhaps they will kill you also. You had better go.'

"Manning said, 'You tell me this because you wish to leave me.'

"I said, 'No, you have plenty of flour which the savages will take – you take what money you have & go to Alexis.'

"Another woman, Ah-tit, came & said, 'Don't stop, come with me.'

"I went with her about 50 yards – heard a shot – looked round & saw Manning lying on the ground. Tahpit (the prisoner) has previously been a long time on the ground. (It appears to have been formerly a constant camping place of Tahpit & his tribe, but Manning had driven them off, & taken possession of the spring. – MBB) I had seen him there the same day but had not said anything.

"I saw him kill Manning – It was a little above the house, outside – I returned into the house after the murder to fetch my blankets but the Indians had taken everything. I saw & examined the body twice. It was afterwards dragged to the water by my brother Liscallum. The house was full of Indians – I don't know how many – they were from Puntzeen & Tatla Lake. At Tatla there is not I think any chief. There were no Homalco Indians there."

Begbie asked the prisoner Tahpit if he had any question to ask. Tahpit said, 'These are lies. Some of the words of this woman are true and some are not true.' He then proceeded to give a statement clearly admitting his guilt, but laying the whole blame on Annahim – who he said was there. (However, I understood his statement before it got translated into English, and stopped it before it got to the jury. – MBB)

Il-se-dlout-nell, another Native woman, also gave sworn testimony, through interpreters, at Tahpit's trial:

"Was at Manning's house the day of the murder. Saw the prisoner there. Two Indians went from the lodge to kill Manning. I and two other women went to get wood. The men were Annahim & Tahpit. I heard Tahpit say, 'All the Indians urge me to kill Manning & Annahim does so too.' That was all I heard. They both had guns. I heard a shot fired presently. Did not see who fired. Both the men (prisoner & Annahim)

WILLIAM MANNING: Fenced land at the proposed junction of the roads from Bute Inlet and Bella Coola, with the intention of trading with miners and pack train crews en route to and from the gold fields of the Cariboo.

TAHPIT: *'Takut' … said to be an 'otter person.'*

ALEX MACDONALD: *Interior trader. Hired by Waddington to start a road from the interior toward the Bute route.*

went straight towards Manning's house. I saw Manning's body – it was quite dead – There were many Indians there. Prisoner Tahpit was among them."

"The prisoner being asked if he had any questions to ask, merely said, 'The words of the woman are true.' "

Scene IV. Lake Nicootlem

REVEREND LUNDIN BROWN: "Scarcely had the good people of Victoria got over the excitement of the tidings brought by Mr. Whymper of these wholesale murders, than more intelligence reached them of fresh crimes committed by the same Indians in a more distant part of the continent."

About three weeks after the events in the Homathko Canyon, a party of miners and packers was en route to the Cariboo gold fields via the "Bentinck Arm route," a road blazed and cleared at about the same time as Waddington's. The pack train had ascended the "precipice" at the head of the Bella Coola valley, and had just crossed into Tsîilhqotin country. The leader of the party was Alexander MacDonald.

REVEREND BROWN: "On the evening of May 21st, MacDonald's party reached the shore of Lake Nicootlem, and prepared to camp there that night ...

"The truth of my narrative, however, compels the mention of [a] woman. Klymtedza's parents were of the Nicootlem tribe, and at the moment of her arrival with the train on the one side of the lake, her relatives were encamped on the other. Accordingly, as night fell, she stole away from the whites, to go to see her people ... 'Chilhowhoaz,' said [Klatsassan], 'see your daughter ... She wears a gown now, instead of, as before, a blanket or a deerskin; she has on shoes instead of moccasins, her hair is combed and well greased. But, chief, she is no longer good – not as a Red man's wife is good ... A few years from now, the man she lives with will leave her, and then what will become of her? She can never be an Indian's wife afterwards. No; she will become a bad thing, or, perhaps (best thing she can do), will use rope [*i.e.* hang herself]. This is what happens to all white men's squaws. They die. Our families consume away. We are all dying off together. The whites want to destroy us. They have ruined our families. They have taken our country from us. They have built their stone houses and towns. They have put their fire-vomiting steamboats on our lakes and rivers, and frightened away the salmon. They have set their vile ploughs in our sacred soil.

KLYMTEDZA: *Tsîlhqot'in country wife of Peter McDougall. Killed by the Tsîlhqotin for betraying them to the pack train.*

"Klymtedza was not long in discovering that the Indians had determined to capture the mule-train … on reaching the packers' camp … She advised them to abandon their train and provisions, and to make their escape on horseback to the coast. … They resolved to move to a hill commanding the neighbourhood. Here they dug a pit breast-deep, in which they placed their goods and *aparejos*, and then occupied it …

"Here they remained accordingly for two days, the Indians meanwhile watching them closely from their camp … MacDonald's patience became fairly exhausted. Calling an Indian to the foot of the knoll, he asked him what they wanted? The Indian replied, with the most nonchalant air, 'We want nothing. You can go on.' … So it was proposed that they should return to Nicootlem, and take up their quarters in an Indian stockade, which was near the lake. This plan was strongly opposed by the squaw. 'No!' said she, 'that plan is bad; if you go from here at all, go on horseback, and straight to the coast. Don't move a step with the train.'

"[But] they took everything with them, and moved slowly and noisily, with their great pack-train, towards the spot where their deadly enemies lay concealed."

"Tom, an Indian," gave sworn testimony in the case of *Regina v. Klatsassine & Piell or Pierre, arising from the murder of Alexander MacDonald*. From Judge Begbie's trial notes, September 29, 1864:

PIELLE: *Also 'Piell', 'Pierre', 'Biyil'. Lha tses'in's son.*

" 'I am of Alexis' tribe. I was employed by MacDonald to look after his horses in the packtrain. … I saw MacDonald killed. The train was turned towards Bella Coola. The Indians were in ambush on each side of the trail. At the first fire MacDonald was wounded (Klatsassine then, in this, killed him). Achink thus killed Higgins dead the first fire. Then

LHA TSES'IN'S DAUGHTER:
Said to have been kidnapped,
raped and then sold back to
her father for $100 by the road
crew; stolen, according to
Chartres Brew, by the
Euclataw and ransomed by
her father for six blankets, two
muskets and a canoe; and
offered, according to Lundin
Brown, to Cox by Lha tses'in
in return for Lha tses'in's
freedom.

all the footmen were killed & the horsemen ran. Piell then fired and killed MacDonald's horse – he ran a short distance on foot. Ya-hoot-la fired & wounded him – he fell on his back with a pistol in his hand. Tshin-kan-lenee came up to finish him but MacDonald shot him. Then Klatsassine fired and broke both his arms. I-shen then fired & killed him dead. That was the last shot.' After that the savages collected all the horses from the woods – They could not find them all for Annahim's party had hidden the horses in the wood. All that Klatsassine's party found were divided among the Indians equally. 'I saw MacDonald after he was dead. The Indians did nothing to the body. Five white men escaped. Klatsassine then took me with him. The attack took place a little on this side of Nacoonthoon."

The white men killed with MacDonald were Clifford Higgins and Peter McDougall.

Reverend Lundin Brown concludes: "The reader will wish to know what became of Klymtedza … She died a violent death."

ACT III

Scene I. New Westminster

FREDERICK SEYMOUR:
Succeeded James Douglas as
governor of the mainland
colony of British Columbia in
1864, two weeks before the
hostilities. Formerly lieu-
tenant-governor of British
Honduras.

MAY 20 – Governor Frederick Seymour writes to Viscount Edward Cardwell, Duke of Newcastle, Secretary of State for the Colonies:

"My main reliance for the capture of the murderers and vindication of the law is in a mounted expedition which I have ordered to be dispatched from Alexandria on the upper Fraser …

"Mr. William Cox, one of the Gold Commissioners of the Cariboo will command a force of about 50 men – sworn constables also, for we wish to proceed legally – a formidable body, safe in the plains against Indian attack. I have been obliged to leave very much to Mr. Cox's discretion but it is believed that he will at once proceed to the head quarters of Alexis, the great Chief of the Chilcoaten tribe, show his warrant and explain that the Queen's Law must have its Course …

"I wish to impress upon Y.G. that there is as yet, no war, I have rejected all offers of assistance from men bent on revenge. I aim at securing justice only."

Seymour then instructed William Cox to hire Donald McLean as his second-in-command.

THE BRITISH COLUMBIAN, MAY 21 – (Editorial by John Robson, later premier of BC)· "We are quite aware that there are those amongst us who are disposed to ignore altogether the rights of the Indian and their claims upon us – who hold the American doctrine of "manifest destiny" in the most fatal form, and say that the native tribes will die off to make way for the Anglo-Saxon race, and the quicker the better; and under the shadow of the unchristian doctrine, the cry for "extermination" is raised at every pretext. Very different however, are the views and sentiments held in reference to the Indians by the British Government. The representatives of the Government may not, in every instance, faithfully delineate the Imperial mind in this respect …

"Depend on it, for every acre of land we obtain by improper means we will have to pay for dearly in the end, and every wrong committed upon those poor people will be visited on our heads."

MAY 24 – Governor Seymour invited all the tribes from the Fraser and Thompson Rivers to celebrate the Queen's birthday. Fifty-seven chiefs and more than 1,000 Indians arrive at New Westminster, and many presents were distributed. Seymour then leaves for Bute Inlet on the vessel, the *Forward*.

Donald McLean

Scene II. Victoria

THE BRITISH COLONIST, JUNE 2 – "EMERGENCY MEETING: Mr. C. B. Young said … justice had not been meted out to the natives. He approved of punishment … But on the other hand, justice should be even handed. Their potato patches at Bentinck Arm had been appropriated by white men and fenced in. Was that justice? … At Nanaimo an Indian Reservation had been made; a cricket ground was wanted, it was formed of the reservation. Was that justice?"

JUNE 11 – "A prayer was offered: 'Lord restrain the vengeance of the

'CHEELA': *A fictional character in Maud Emery's novel,* A River of Tears, *based on Pielle's real-life Homalco wife, whose name does not come down to us. In the novel, 'Cheela' is raped by a member of the road crew, which contributes to the emotions already running high against the intruders.*

savage and bring speedily to an end the blood thirstiness of professing Christians.' "

Scene III. The Chilcotin Plateau

JUNE 12 – Cox and his expedition, consisting mostly of American miners, arrives at Puntzi Lake. Cox finds Manning's body and has a fort built and a white flag flown.

JUNE 18 – Governor Seymour, Inspector Chartres Brew and others arrive at Bentinck Arm aboard HMS *Sutlej*. Brew hires 30 Bella Coola packers, and the party proceeds eastward to rendezvous with Cox and his expedition at Puntzi Lake. Shortly after entering Chilcotin country, the party comes across the corpses from MacDonald's party.

JULY 7-10 – At Puntzi Lake, Chartres Brew discovers that Nancy has remained at Manning's farm. Brew asks her to act as an emissary, and persuade Tsilhqot'in Chief Alexis to come and parlay. "Nancy," Governor Seymour reported in a dispatch to Cardwell, "came backwards and forwards once or twice, brought in some children, then one man, who seemed to test the sincerity of our profession of moderation. When he had returned unharmed, a considerable number of squaws formed a fishing station 6 miles off and entered the camp almost daily with growing confidence to barter trout for sugar. … Fully satisfied at last of our good faith the women promised that Alexis should come in, if the Governor remained, and then finally departed in search of him."

Then: "Alexis and his men come on at the best pace of their horses holding their muskets over their heads to show they come in peace. Having ascertained which was the Governor, the chief threw himself from his horse, and at once approached us. He was dressed in a French uniform such as one sees in the picture of Montcalm.

Seymour quotes Alexis as saying: " … the great chiefs have lost much of their authority since the Indians hear every white man assume the distinction … the men under Klatsassan and Tellot have renounced all connection … and have a right to make war on us without it being any affair of his." They were "des marvais sauvages, qui connaissent pas de bon Dieu."

When Alexis asked Seymour how long he would remain on his hunting grounds, Seymour said, "Three years!" However, he left the interior and returned to the coast. In a further dispatch to Cardwell, Seymour wrote: "[T]here was no use shutting my eyes to the fact that this was a war – merciless on their side – in which we were engaged with the Chilcotin nation and must be carried on as a war by us." Later, he states: "The Chilcotins are not murderers."*

* 'Colonial Correspondence,' July to October, 1864, in the BC Archives.

Scene IV. In the hills above Eagle Lake

JULY 17 – Impatient with Cox's orders to remain in the fort, Donald McLean and a Shuswap Indian scout the countryside for the Tsîlhqot'in. In their oral tradition, McLean is known as Samandlin. His fate, which is considered by them as crucial to the Tsîlhqot'in victory, was described, more than a century later, by Tsîlhqot'in elder Eugene William.

" 'He find the trail all right, that Samandlin,' says Eugene.

" 'Then somebody, he take out his knife out of its sheath, and cut from kind of a tree, right down on the trail. Leave 'em on a trail.'

"At this point, Eugene takes a firm hold of his knife, holds his thumb against the dull edge of the blade to steady his hand, and cuts a thin slice from the stick he's whittling. He takes the strip he's cut and puts it on the ground in front of him.

" 'He put it on the trail,' he says, pointing with his knife to the strip of wood on the ground between his feet. …

" 'So Samandlin come there, and he's a long time on the trail, I guess. …

" 'He wanted to find out how long ago that one there. So he put it in his mouth.

"'Pretty soon, somebody … bang. Over there.'

"Eugene points towards the trees out behind the cabin.

"'Well, that first one, I guess he miss. Two guys. So the second one, he shot him, Samandlin."*

* Glavin *et al.*, *Nemiah: The Unconquered Country.*

Scene V. The encampment of the expeditionary force

JULY 30 – Chief Alexis and Tahpit's son, Joe, bring a message from Lha

SIT'AX: *Also Setah or Set'ax, a Tsîlhqot'in medicine man, captured by the Homalco and returned as an adult to join his people. He was employed in work on the road and it is thought that he tried to stop the massacre. Possibly the man known as Chraychanurd who warned Qwhittie to run home.*

CHEDEKKI: *Tsîlhqot'in man employed by the whites packing heavy blasting drills.*

* The *British Columbian*, August 24, 1864.

tses'in that if the whites would remain where they were, "then Klattsassan and Tellot would gather all the murderers and give themselves up."

Cox, in his testimony at the trial, said: "I answered that we should do just as we thought fit – that I should be glad to see them if they would come in – but if not, that I would follow up and kill men, women and children."

AUGUST 10 – Lha tses'in sends Tom to Cox with a gift of money and word that a party of men will arrive in four days. Cox responds that "No harm will come to them and I will hand them over to the 'Big Chief'."* Cox means Begbie.

AUGUST 12 – Tom returns with Cox's gift of tobacco to Lha tses'in, who thinks the "Big Chief" means Seymour.

AUGUST 15 – At 8:30 in the morning, Lha tses'in, with eight Chilcotin men and their families, arrive with Chief Alexis and some of his men.

LUNDIN BROWN: "They came into camp unarmed, save with knives. They looked very fearsome and defiant. The idea of having come here to be killed was evidently the farthest from those fierce and fearless faces."

LHA TSES'IN: "I have brought 7 murderers and I am one myself. I return 1 horse, 1 mule and $20 for the Governor as a token of good faith. The names of the men present are: myself, Tellot, Chee-loot, Tapitt, Piem, Chessus, Cheddekki and Sangtanki. 10 more are at large. 3 others dead."*

LUNDIN BROWN: "They were ordered to give up their knives. As soon as the order was understood, an expression of hesitancy and alarm came over them. As for Klatsassan, he refused point blank to give up his. 'Take it from him' ... 2 stout Californians came forward ... He shook them off ... drew the knife, and dashed it to the floor. Irons were then brought, and their hands and ankles fettered."

Wochess handed Cox an ounce and half of gold dust. Chessus handed over $550 in silver.

COX: "I wish to inform you that in the name of the Queen I am placing you under arrest. You are my prisoners."

LHA TSES'IN: "Where is the Great Chief English?"

CHIEF ALEXIS: "Mr. Cox must speak with 2 tongues."

TELLOT: "King George men are great liars."[*]

Commissioner William Cox, in sworn testimony before Judge Matthew Baillie Begbie, September 28, 1864, provided the following account of the "surrender" of Lha tses'in and the others:

"I was in charge of the expedition to whom these prisoners surrendered. A message had come in from Klatsassine to Mr. Brew's camp and mine. It was to the effect that if we would not follow them to the mountains any more they would come and give themselves up to us. … Afterwards they sent money as a test of their good faith. Klatsassine said that he had come to [offer] his body to save his wives and children. I said they must come in otherwise I would keep on until the snow. I promised them that I would not hurt them in my camp, that I had no power to kill them, that I would hand them over to the big chief (meaning me – I think the Indians believed it to be His Excellency whose photograph was shown them at this time, but not by Mr. Cox. – MBB).

"Two days afterward they came in, in a row & sat down. I said nothing to them & waited some time. At length Alexis said something to Klatsassine who addressing me said, We are seven murderers who are here to give ourselves up, & I am another. (They dared not shoot or light a fire for fear of pursuit.) They thought best to give themselves up in order to save the lives of their wives and children. I made them thoroughly understand that they were prisoners. They were put into an enclosure. When they were legally examined on the 26th Sept. they were cautioned in the statutory form and made statements, Klatsassine to the effect "There is no murderer here, – but we assisted." Telloot said he have lived with the whites and liked them – and was sorry when they were murdered. These 8 however (who surrendered 15 Aug. – MBB) were all included in making up the number of 21 Indians who were

[*] Col. William Byers, the *British Columbian*, September 7, 1864.

engaged in the murder. There was no inducement whatever to the Indians to come in – it was entirely voluntary on their part."

On September 7, the *British Colonist* reported: "The account given by our informant of the means by which Mr. Cox obtained possession of the eight Indian prisoners … does not look very well."

A meeting between the Horse Indians and a government party near Lillooet, 1864 or '65. Foreground, right to left: Governor Seymour, Seymour's secretary Arthur Birch, Sir Lambton Loraine, and Lt. Admiral Elliot, chief magistrate of the district.

CHAPTER 6

'As to the Very Important Topic of Surrender ...'

AFTER THE ARREST, COMMISSIONER COX held the prisoners in the stockade until reinforcements arrived for the move to Quesnellemouth. The prisoners were allowed to have their families, and Lha tses'in's youngest wife brought two children with her.

LUNDIN BROWN: "While they were in camp there were ever a pair of watchful eyes on the prisoners, lest they should escape. So it happened that some of their peculiar customs were noted. For instance, in the middle of the night, the Indian mothers, Toowaewoot amongst the rest would rise, remove their infants from their baskets, and unbind them. Then taking water into their mouths (probably to take off the chill) they would proceed to squirt it forth over the papoos, and so wash it from head to foot. Next they would pour a whole basketful of water over it, then dry it, put it back in its cradle. This was done at midnight. How they guessed the time nobody could imagine."

While Brew attempted to capture the rest of the fugitives, the prisoners were moved to Quesnellemouth to be tried by Judge Begbie, who wrote the following letter dated September 30, 1864 to Governor Seymour:

TOOWAEWOOT: *Lha tses'in's young second wife, whom he took after defeating her father in battle.*

"Dear Sir:

"I send you by this post copy of my notes at the trial of the Indian prisoners here. There can be no doubt of the guilty complicity of the 5 prisoners in all the murders – as they must be considered – in the eye of the law – and I should think, in a common sense view too, even making allowances for the ignorance and habits of the prisoners.

"As to the very important topic of the surrender of the prisoners, you will find Mr. Cox's statement in the note of *Regina v. Teloot* and others. I received your letter of the 21st inst. this morning, after all the business was concluded – and although the matter had already been to some extent inquired into at the trial, I thought it as well to examine Klatsassine, who had acted as spokesman at the surrender, in private as to his views on the matter. I only took (of course) the interpreter Baptiste – nobody was present who could understand him but myself; and I mentioned to no person the object of my enquiry. Of course I told Mr. Gaggin, whom I consider to be in charge of the prisoners (though upon this point, and upon others respecting the police altogether in this neighbourhood, and payment of expenses … some doubt or misapprehension appears to exist). Mr. Gaggin accompanied me to the place of confinement.

"Both Mr. Cox and Klatsassine leave me under the impression – in fact they explicitly state that the latter was completely in the dark as to the consequences of his entering Mr. Cox's camp on the 15th August.

"But it is to be observed that Klatsassine nowhere, either in court nor today charges any breach of faith in Mr. Cox – Klatsassine I think suspects Alexis (a rival chief, who had everything to gain, both by receiving an immediate reward, renewing tranquility, and removing a competitor for influence) of duplicity while he acted as interpreter – as he did during the negotiations before the interview and also (I think) at the first interview with Mr. Cox at all events. Mr. Cox seems to think that blame may perhaps be attributed to another channel either solely, or jointly with Alexis. After Baptiste and Fitzgerald were in camp there is no doubt that everything was thoroughly understood by Klatsassine, except that I

MATTHEW BAILLIE BEGBIE:
Sworn in as the first judge for the court of British Columbia in 1858. He later received a knighthood.

think he believed he was to have the honour of an interview with your excellency instead of with me. (But he was then a prisoner and the explanation came rather late.) In answer to my question, whether he would have come in if he had known that he was henceforth to be in confinement for the murder of these men, he gave a decided negative. But when I put the matter to him in the light mentioned by Mr. Cox in his evidence, 'What then would you have done? – you had no flour – you could not hunt – you had no fish – you could not light a fire – must you not have come in soon on any terms?' he gave a very frank affirmative reply. In short, I think that if they were not fairly hunted down on the 15th August, they were on the very verge of being so: and I think they grasped at the idea of a conference; to which perhaps they were encouraged by the gift on the part of Mr. Cox (previous to the 15th Aug.) in the last message he sent them of a couple of pieces of tobacco. This Klatsassine said they brought with them to Mr. Cox's camp and smoked it there (probably did so in the interval of silence mentioned by Mr. Cox in his evidence) then, said Klatsassine, we thought ourselves safe. We have all heard of the sacredness of the pipe of peace on the Eastern side among the Indians – I never had any experience on the matter here – in fact there has been no opportunity – this is the first case of anything approaching to a war that has occurred since 1850. Mr. Cox probably as unthinking as I should have been, tells me he never noticed it at all. The other point upon which they were certainly misled, either by their own hopes, or by the promises of some unauthorized agent, was, that they were to be allowed, until my arrival, to camp where they pleased. This was certainly their impression – and very disagreeably disturbed they must have felt when Mr. Cox refused to allow them to depart, but detained them on that first night, and in fact ever since. Alexis also, I am informed was of the same opinion: when he heard that they wished to camp with him that night, but that Mr. Cox would not let them, 'then' said he, 'Mr. Cox must have two tongues.'

"It is a very annoying circumstance. Klatsassine however never said so to me (in reference to Mr. Cox) and I think he would have done so, if he had thought so.

"The whole of the prisoners were terribly afraid during the trial. I think they kept back nothing. I think they would tell the exact truth, either to you or to me.

"I was particular in inquiring into the name of the individual who as they all assert and I have not the least doubt, truly, was by his rash threat the cause of all this uproar, and of the deaths of 21 white men & 3 Indians, already, and nobody can say how many more by the hand of the executioner and famine in the fall and winter. From today's conversation with Klatsassine I have introduced one or two items of description – 'fair' – 'not an old man' – 'returned to V. by the steamer' 'like Lieut. Stewart' – It was not Brewster, nor any of his party – the threat acquired substance and force from the circumstance that the same threat is said to have been made to them previous to the smallpox of /62-/63. When half their numbers (on a moderate computation) perished.

"Baptiste and Fitzgerald make famous interpreters. The latter is of course unnecessary to those who speak French.

"These assizes have only decided the fate (as far as I am concerned) of 5 of the 8 prisoners. Chidekki was only tried on one indictment – was not recognized by any witness – It is said Peterson can swear to him. I believe he goes below for trial at New Westminster. You can enquire into the matter from him there, and respite the 5 here (or Klatsassine, who conducted the negotiations can be sent down to you with Baptiste and Ogilvy). That will at all events be cheaper than having them sent down to N.W. for trial, as the witnesses etc. will not have to go.

"The remaining two prisoners, Tnanawki and his son Cheloot, I intimated might be set at large. (They have been at large for the last 10 days). There is no specific charge against them – nothing at all except Klatsassine's saying at his first interview with Mr. Cox which, I need not say, is no legal evidence against them whatever. Moreover all the prisoners, who I believe speak truth as in the presence of a higher power, exonerate them from all participation in anything we could call a murder, in any Chilcotin construction of the word. They were neither at Brewster's camp, nor Manning's, nor MacDonald's – they are stated to have been present at the quasi-skirmish where McLean lost his life where, says Mr. Cox. 'We fired at them, they fired at us' – and there is not the least evidence that either of them fired the fatal shot (there) or fired at all.

"As to the latter part of your letter (about local excitement) where you quote from Mr. Cardwell – I think that is best answered by the fact that all these 8 prisoners have been brought a long distance without any attempt at mob law, or even an insult. Three of them were virtually acquitted on a court where I certainly thought the evidence very slight, notwithstanding the moral certitude that we all had of their actual complicity. Two of them are at large on parole in the streets of the town unmolested. All the 5 convicts have confessed their guilt of capital offenses (generally &) of the offenses for which they have been convicted in particular.

"The conviction of Telloot would not be followed, in England, by execution: at least where others suffered capitally for the same offence. Pielle is young – very mild-looking, much under the influence of Klatsassine. (But he shot MacDonald's horse, riding away.) Klatsassine is the finest savage I have met with yet, I think. But I believe also he has fired more shots than any of them. It seems horrible to hang 5 men at once – especially under the circumstances of the capitulation. Yet the blood of 21 whites calls for retribution. And these fellows are cruel murdering pirates taking life and making slaves in the same spirit in which you or I would go out after partridges or rabbit shooting. 'Squint Eye's' tribe is nearly annihilated by them. Klatsassine shoots MacDonald as he lies on the ground, distributes his horses, and carries off his servant 'Tom' as a slave.

"I do not envy you your task of coming to a decision.

"Believe me, yours truly

"Matt. Begbie"

At the end of his trial notes, Begbie states: "All the prisoners being brought into court, I told them, that having seen them and examined the complaints about them, I had become convinced that they had each of them killed or were engaged in killing white men – I asked them what their law was against murderers? – They replied Death. I said our law just the same. That they were guilty of death – why should it not be pronounced?"

Lha tses'in replied: "I have killed whites. I was induced to do so by Tyookell, who gave me a gun to do so.

"A white man took all our names down in a book last spring & told us we should all die, whose names were down, of smallpox. Tyookell told us this would certainly happen unless we killed every white man – It was at Homalco – the white man who said this came in the steamer – he is not killed – he returned in the steamer to Victoria – he is not old – he has fair hair – like Lieut. Stewart whom we saw in Mr. Cox's camp. Yahootla and his brother were bad Indians irritating the white men with their thefts.

"Five Indians were present when the white man on the steamer took down the names. That was the reason of the outbreak."*

* Transcript of the handwritten trial notes of Judge Begbie. Quotation marks and some punctuation have been added.

CHAPTER 7

'A Question of Colonial Importance'

QUESNELLEMOUTH, OCTOBER 2, 1864 – Reverend Lundin Brown: "We went to the prison, Baptiste and I, and found it to be no regular gaol but an improvised affair, a mere log house, with part partitioned off for a cell. Here were the unhappy prisoners, sitting squatting on the floor … all heavily shackled … They said, 'They meant war, not murder.' "

NEW WESTMINSTER, OCTOBER 4 – Governor Seymour writes to Cardwell, the Colonial Secretary: "The Indian insurrection is merely referred to by me as a … question of colonial importance. I would, however, beg most respectfully to point out, that should a real war take place between the Indian population and the whites, the former numbering 60,000 and the latter 7,000, I may find myself compelled to follow in the footsteps of the Governor of Colorado … and invite every white man to shoot every Indian he may meet. Such a proclamation would not be badly received here in the case of an emergency."

QUESNELLEMOUTH, OCTOBER 26 – Lundin Brown described the hanging of the Tsîlhqot'in prisoners: "The executive, it appeared,

FACING PAGE: *Governor Seymour in Lillooet, 1865. One of the two men behind Mrs. Seymour is Lillooet Chief Silko Salish. Arthur Birch, Seymour's secretary, is at the far right.*

thought not of mercy … As they went I shook hands with each one, bidding them farewell …

"The next thing I noticed was some one offering Klatsassan drink, and his refusing. I don't think he saw me looking, or that he refused the liquor from any notion save a sense of [the] impropriety of the thing, and a heroic kind of feeling …

"The prisoners were then led on to the scaffold … a voice was heard; it was Tapeet. He first called out to his comrades to 'have courage.' Then he spoke two sentences to the Indians round the scaffold. 'Tell the Chilcotins to cease anger against the whites.'

"One instant more and the signal was given; the drops fell. All was done so quietly and so quickly that it was difficult to realize that the frightful work was over.

"The remains were interred with Christian burial, after the Anglican rite, in a wood near Quesnellemouth, not far from the Cariboo road. A wooden cross with a rude inscription was set up to mark the spot where these poor fellows sleep."

Chedekki was not condemned with the others. In his deposition to Baptiste Demerest, regarding the incidents on the Homathko, he had said: "When the whites would be eating, they would give a bit of food to the children and the man in charge [Brewster] would take it away and throw it into the fire."

En route to his trial in New Westminster he escaped into the mountains, and was never recaptured.

LONDON, DECEMBER 1 – Cardwell, the Colonial Secretary, responds to Governor Seymour's October 4 correspondence: "I do not understand the meaning of the paragraph in which you speak of inviting every white man to shoot every Indian he might meet. I can rely on your continued adherence to the line of conduct hitherto pursued by you, which appears to have been perfectly consistent with humanity and good policy."

In 1865, Ahan and Lutas, two Tsîlhqot'in men who had eluded capture in 1864, were pursuaded by Chief Annahim to surrender themselves into the custody of trader Morris Moss, who was deputized by Colonial Constable John Ogilvy for that purpose. Ahan and Lutas were taken to New Westminster and tried by Judge H. P. P. Crease. The *British Columbian* of July 4, 1865 reports that Judge Crease advised the grand jury that their job was to "unravel the last tangled skein of bloodshed and murder which had enveloped the Bute Inlet and Chilcotin territory" the previous summer. He told the jurors that the entire story behind the causes of the uprising would never be known, but the jury should consider "the horror felt by the Indians for the small-pox, and their resulting fear and hatred of white men."

Both Ahan and Lutas were convicted. Ahan was hanged, but Governor Seymour pardoned Lutas.

Alfred Waddington approached the colony's Legislative Council with a claim for compensation. He petitioned to be allowed to surrender his charter, and to be reimbursed for the expenses he incurred attempting to build the Bute Inlet road to the Cariboo. He argued that he had not been afforded any protection by the colonial government. Governor Seymour responded that no such protection had been requested, the government was not notified that the road-builders were in that particular locality, and besides, it was murder, and not war, and no state could guarantee its citizens against murder.

The total cost of the expeditionary force against the Tsilhqot'in had amounted to about $80,000. Notwithstanding their dismissal of Waddington's claim, during the legislative session of 1864-65 the Legislative Council passed a resolution to request the British government to bear half the expenses of the Chilcotin War, as the affair had come to be called. On July 22, 1865, Cardwell refused to assist in the costs, on the grounds that the expedition had been demanded locally, "as an act of retributive justice, and as being needful for the safety of all persons who might be engaged hereafter in similar undertakings," and as a consequence, Her Majesty's Government was in no way responsible for the costs. The Legislative Council granted Donald McLean's widow an annuity of $100 a year for five years.

Chartres Brew, in the coroner's report he filed with the colonial government following his investigation of the massacre in Bute Inlet, concluded: "All the time it was known that the Indians were little removed from a state of starvation yet not the slightest effort was made to obtain their good will or guard against their enmity. When they worked they complained Brewster paid them badly and gave them nothing to eat. They got orders for powder, balls, clothes or blankets. They never took provisions in payment: they thought they had a right to be fed, but were not ... The women were better fed as the price of prostitution was enough to eat."

Waddington clung to his idea of a route to British Columbia's interior, and went to Ottawa to try to raise interest in a rail line through the mountains that witnessed the events of 1864.

On February 29, 1872, Victoria's *British Colonist* newspaper noted:

"One afternoon in the middle of February, he [Alfred Waddington] was standing in the reception room of Russell House, conversing with some railway magnates respecting his great Bute Inlet railway scheme, when a physician of Ottawa approached, and seizing the old gentleman by both hands, shook them warmly, saying, 'I have just left the worst case of confluent smallpox I have ever seen.'

"Mr. Waddington instantly withdrew his hands from (as it afterward appeared) the infected grasp of the indiscreet medical man and sat down, trembling violently. A few days afterward the poor gentleman was seized with the smallpox, which soon carried him off."

Interior chiefs at New Westminster, 1864 or '66: Na Mah (Dog Creek), Quibquarlse
(Alkali Lake), Tao'task (Canoe Creek), Se-as-kut (Shuswap), Timpt Khan (Babine
Lake), Silko Salish (Lillooet), William (William's Lake), Kam-co-Saltze (Soda Creek),
Sosastumpt (Bridge Creek).

CHAPTER 8

A Mirror of War

The hanging of the Tsilhqot'in Chiefs in 1864 is a tragedy which, if we
are to move forward with respect and in good faith, must be recognized.
– British Columbia Attorney General Colin
Gablemann, at a meeting with the Cariboo-
Tsilhqot'in leadership at Toosey, October 28, 1993

IN 1993 ROSA HO, CURATOR at the University of British Columbia's
Museum of Anthropology, invited me to create an installation of the
paintings, sculptures and book-works generated by my upcoast and
archival explorations. At the same time the events of the 1860s had
become, in the media, what they had always been to the native people
– a current event.

The 1994 exhibition, *HIGH SLACK*, was not solely "about" the
Chilcotin War. My interest in the issue of parallel realities had first been
raised by the contrasting 1792 journals of George Vancouver and the
Spanish captains Galiano and Valdés. It had been reinforced by Hom-
fray's report of his being examined by the Tsilhqot'in man in the
Homathko Canyon for signs of a similar humanity. This became the

hub of the work. Around it, I made stations from which one could look at the native/white/landscape concurrence from different viewpoints.

I did not think I should ask the descendants of those involved to validate my point of view, but I did think I should provide them with an opportunity to speak to the historical subject matter. With their input, Rosa Ho, Greg Brass and I organized a symposium, "The Tsilhqot'in War of 1864 and the 1993 Cariboo-Chilcotin Justice Inquiry." On November 19, 1994, 150 people gathered in the First Nations House of Learning at UBC. Over half of these were native people, many from the Interior. Appropriately, I had almost lost my voice, and could barely speak.

The native people presented their stories of the events of the 1860s – theirs to tell and, hopefully, theirs soon to share. Thomas Billyboy, Tsîl-hqot'in chief from 'Esdilagh, rearranged the tone of the day's approach to information by telling us that the names of people involved in the war are in, and of, the land, come about through people's lives, and were themselves powerful.

Annie Williams, former chief of the Nemiah Band, provided the key to the door that had been shut on the causes of the war from the Tsîl-hqot'in point of view. She made it clear that they did not talk about the war easily in public. It is not an everyday topic but told only in quiet times. Every native person however who did speak about the events of 1864 emphasized that it was a war and the Tsîlqot'in did not lose.

Judge Cunliffe Barnett, who grew up at his father's Forbes Bay logging operation at Ahpokum, has been a provincial court judge based in Williams Lake for twenty years. He stated:

"My real education began when I arrived in Williams Lake. I learned how the justice system has misunderstood the native people. Begbie, in the 1864 trial, overlooked necessary material and bent the rules. John Barnston, the lawyer who was supposed to defend the prisoners, had an interest in pushing a road through from Bella Coola. That Crease tried the men in New Westminster was outrageous as he was at the time the attorney-general of the province. Even Begbie thought this was odd."

Barnett said that in his opinion, "The men who were hanged should be pardoned."

Judge Anthony Sarich had led the Cariboo-Chilcotin Justice Inquiry, a provincial government commission established to investigate the roots of the poor relationship between the native people and the justice system in BC's interior. One of Sarich's key findings during the inquiry hearings concerned the questionable actions of the colonial forces in securing the capture of the Tsîlhqot'in leaders in 1864 and the appropriateness of various aspects of their trial at Quesnellemouth. In his report, Sarich states: "Whatever the correct version, that episode of history has left a deep wound in the body of Chilcotin society. It is time to heal that wound. Since that trial and those hangings occurred before British Columbia joined Confederation, it is appropriate that Victoria grant a posthumous pardon to those chiefs, and I so recommend."

The attorney-general sent José Villa-Arce to speak about what action had been undertaken on the recommendations of the Sarich report. Villa-Arce, a senior policy analyst with the attorney-general's Aboriginal Justice Unit, again addressed the question of which level of government should deal with the issue of a pardon – the federal or provincial government – on the grounds that British Columbia is now a province, and that Canada is not constituted as it was then. The government appeared to be doing what it does best, slipping behind rules and regulations, stalling. Members of the audience told him they wanted the graves, now under a hospital parking lot, marked, that they wanted a full pardon from the minister of justice, and their own police force. They suggested that the Sarich inquiry was just a big show.

At lunch a BC Appeals Court judge told me it was the first time he had ever heard native people speak in public. He was overwhelmed by the eloquence. "I just deal with pieces of paper," he said.

Near the end of the afternoon, a figure rose to the microphone and said:

"My name is Mel Rothenburger. There is a lot of talk about apologies, and I want to know, who will apologize for the shooting of my great-grandfather in the back?"

There was silence. Rothenburger's book, *The Chilcotin War*, had been used as a text in the schools of BC's interior, and every Tsîlhqot'in person in the room knew that his great-grandfather was Donald McLean. Rothenburger sat down amid a hiss of hostility.

Roger William, the young chief of the Nemiah Band, restored balance by speaking of a middle way. He spoke in both English and Tsîlhqot'in so those of his people who did not speak English and who would be watching the afternoon's events later on videotape, would understand what was said.

The day's speakers all affirmed a direct connection between the present mistrust of the justice system by Native people in the province's interior, and the events of 1864. However, the healing of the wound referred to by Sarich is not a "Native" problem; it is the concern and responsibility of all of us.

High slack, when the tide has risen to its highest point and pauses before it ebbs, is not just a good time to fish. I have used it as a metaphor for a pause in ideological currents, a time to collect ourselves and perceive, not just what we have been taught to see and know, but to imagine what might be if our socially-aquired filters evaporated.

During the Renaissance, a famous "mirror of anatomy" called *La Specola* (the double mirror) was constructed so that the *concepts* employed in anatomical speculation could be examined along with the bodies dissected. *High Slack* mirrors both the events of the 1860s *and* the forms in which they are retrievable, so that we (I) can see the changing attitudes of those (I) who write about it.

*Remains of bridge on Waddington's road near the site of the
massacre. The photo was taken by a survey crew in 1928.*

Will Bule Wax Surrender Its Secret?

IN THE COASTAL CHANNELS AND INLETS, size, distance, colour and form flicker and transform with light and moisture.

A shadow is seen – not seen; it ripples across the water, darts up the iron canyons, flees before us or lingers behind. It was seen by me in the summers I travelled the inlets; the wax balls, never.

In the springtime of those years, the pollen from the trees was so thick in the water it formed bay-sized rafts of yellow lace and clung, as the tide fell, to the rocks in gold filigree. We would leave Refuge early, the fog oozing out from the lake. The spicy smells of the grass and cottonwood along a river would flash and intoxicate. Stands of fireweed were six feet tall, glaciers burned like opals. We went up … up …

Does the fireweed grow where the moss was soaked with blood? Do I remember or construct? Who has seen the wax balls? Is their substance stored, like violence, in cells or genes? Is the "shadow" I have chased a peopled landscape, or a state of mind?

Artist Corrine Corry likens memory to caustic junctions, that golden lattice of light cast up by the water onto a receptive surface which both affects the form of, and is itself altered by, the light. "History" is the construct of what and how we remember and retrieve.

Graham Greene said each journey was a form of psychoanalysis. I say the inlets are as exotic as Tibet, as true as fiction. Reporting in after my trip up Bute Inlet, I asked Doris Hope if homesteaders in the old days had mentioned Bute Wax.

"Oh yes," she said. "There was that man, Schnarr. His daughters had pet cougars. He used to come down here from Bute, where he trapped, to the store. Once he brought a blob of something from up there to show Norman, and when we started talking he put it on the kitchen counter.

"It got to be quitting time and when the loggers came in to discuss the day's work with Norman I always made them take off their caulk boots – not in my house! By that time, the blob had melted all over the floor and they walked all through it in their socks."

The next summer I asked Doris to tell the story to a visitor. She seemed very surprised and denied having seen any such wax or of having known Schnarr.

FACING PAGE: *Indian bridge at Watsonqua.*

In the morning the fresh snow on the mountains

and the coldness of the air brought tears to my eyes.

SOURCES AND

ACKNOWLEDGMENTS

THE MUSEUM OF ANTHROPOLOGY installation of *HIGH SLACK* contained a desk on which rested a small handbound volume of the historical matrix from which I drew inspiration for the exhibition. Terry Glavin invited me to expand that material into the present book, and he and Rolf Maurer made it possible.

I would like to thank my companions on the voyage: Danny Louie and the late Joe Barnes for the Toba expedition, Susan Pielle, Pete Harry and the late Elizabeth Harry (Keekus), for animating the archives, Rosa Ho for her amazing support and tenacity, Brian Mayne, and Ray Hance for material from Tsîl-hqot'in archives, Greg Brass for organizing the symposium, and the Tsîlhqot'in people, who gave so much of themselves to it.

Thanks to Sam Smythe who made a trip up the Homathko Valley a reality. My husband Bobo Fraser went everywhere with me, and I would not have gone so far without him. John Bovey and Brian Young of the BC Provincial Archives and Records (BCARS) provided me with material from their files. Thanks to The University of British Columbia and the BC Cultural Services Branch for research and art grants.

ILLUSTRATIONS

Page 8: Judy Williams; p. 11: Charles George Horetzky, Vancouver Public Library (VPL) No. 8544; p. 16: University of British Columbia Library, Special Collections; p. 18: British Columbia Archives and Records Service (BCARS) A-

05487; p. 19: BCARS FO-7353; p. 20: Maynard, BCARS A-00903; p. 22: BCARS G-07527; p. 36: UBC Special Collections; p. 38: BCARS A-4126; p. 42: UBC Special Collections; p. 46: Horetzky, BCARS A-4155; p. 49: BCARS P-00109; p. 56: BCARS A-01228; p. 58: BCARS A-02833; p. 59: Royal British Columbia Museum (RBCM) 1860s; p. 62: Vancouver Museum I-1809; p. 64: BCARS F-09011; p. 65: Charles Gentile, RBCM 6198; p. 66: BCARS D-07691; p 70: UBC Special Collections; p. 72: BCARS P-00105; p. 73: BCARS A-02535; p. 74: BCARS A-001127; p. 85: BCARS A-01454; p 91: Gentile, BCARS 95333; p. 93: BCARS A-08953; p. 98: Gentile, National Archives of Canada C-88938; p. 103: Dally, BCARS C-09263; p. 108: UBC Special Collections; p. 111: VPL 8555.

BOOKS AND OTHER SOURCES

British Columbia. *Correspondence Relative to the Discovery of Gold in the Fraser's River District, in British Columbia.* London: Eyre and Spottiswood, 1858.

Begbie, Matthew Baillie. Letter and trial notes sent to Frederick Seymour, September, 1964. Colonial Correspondence, BCARS.

Bouchard, Randy, and Dorothy Kennedy. *Sliammon Life, Sliammon Lands.* Talonbooks, Vancouver, 1983

The *British Colonist*, Victoria, various issues.

The *British Columbian*, New Westminster, various issues.

Brown, Rev. Robert Christopher Lundin. *Klatsassan, and Other Reminiscences of Missionary Life in British Columbia.* London: Society for Promoting Christian Knowledge, 1873.

Duff, Wilson. *The Indian History of British Columbia. Vol 1: The Impact of the White Man.* Victoria: British Columbia Provincial Museum, 1964

Glavin, Terry, and the People of the Nemiah Valley. *Nemiah: The Unconquered Country.* Vancouver: New Star Books, 1992

Grant, George M. *Ocean to Ocean: Sandford Fleming's Expedition Through Canada in 1872.* Sampson, Low, Marston, Low and Searle, London, 1873.

Hewlett, Edward Sleigh. "The Chilcotin Uprising: A Study of Indian-White Relations in Nineteenth Century British Columbia." MA thesis, University of BC, 1972.

Homfray, Robert. "A Winter Journey in 1861," the *Victoria Province*, December 22, 1894.

Lane, Robert Brockstedt. "Cultural Relations of the Chilcotin Indians of West Central British Columbia." PhD thesis, University of Washington, 1953.

Morice, Adrian Gabriel. *The History of the Northern Interior of British Columbia, Formerly New Caledonia.* Toronto: William Briggs, 1904.

Munday, Don. *The Unknown Mountain.* Seattle: The Mountaineers, 1975; reissue Lake Louise, AB: Coyote Books, 1993.

"Origins of the Massacre." Anonymous typescript, BCARS.

Poole, Francis. *Queen Charlotte Islands: A Narrative of Discovery and Adventure in the North Pacific*, ed. John W. Lydon. London: Hurst and Blackett, 1872.

Reinhart, Herman Francis. *The Golden Frontier: The Recollections of Herman Francis Reinhart, 1851-1869*, ed. Doyce B. Nunis Jr. Austin: University of Texas Press, 1962.

Rothenburger, Mel. *The Chilcotin War*. Langley: Mr. Paperback, 1978.

Saunders, Frederick John. "Homatcho, or the Story of the Bute Inlet Expedition and the Massacre by the Chilcoaten Indians." *Resources of British Columbia* 3:1, March 1, 1885. Victoria: Munroe Miller.

A Spanish Voyage to Vancouver and the Northwest Coast of America. Translated by Cecil Jane. London: Argonaut Press, 1930.

"A Survivor's Account." Typescript, BCARS.

Vancouver, George. *A Voyage of Discovery to North America, Vols. I-IV*, ed. W. Kaye Lamb. London: The Hakluyt Society.

Victoria *Daily Chronicle*, various issues.

Walbran, John T. *British Columbia Coast Names: 1592-1906*. Ottawa: Government Printing Bureau, 1909.

Whymper, Frederick. *Travel and Adventure in the Territory of Alaska, Formerly Russian America – Now Ceded to the United States – and in Various Other Parts of the North Pacific*. London: John Murray, 1868.

Williams, Judith. "Whose Story Is This?" Exhibition and catalogue, Surrey Art Gallery, November 1991.

——*HIGH SLACK*. Exhibition, the UBC Museum of Anthropology, Vancouver, June 21, 1994-January 3, 1995.

INDEX

Copyright © 1996 by Judy Williams

Published by New Star Books Ltd. All rights reserved. No part of this work may be repro-
duced or used in any form or by any means – graphic, electronic, or mechanical –
without prior permission. Any request for photocopying or other reprographic copying
must be sent in writing to the Canadian Copyright Licensing Agency (CANCOPY), 900 - 6
Adelaide Street East, Toronto, Ontario M5C 1H6

Please direct submissions and editorial enquiries to: Transmontanus, Box C-25, Fernhill
Road, Mayne Island, B.C. V0N 2J0. All other correspondence, including sales and distri-
bution enquiries, should be directed to New Star Books, 2504 York Avenue, Vancouver,
B.C. V6K 1E3

Transmontanus is edited by Terry Glavin
Cover and series design by Val Speidel
Cover photograph of pictograph of Quodham by Judy Williams
Map by Fiona MacGregor
Produced by Rolf Maurer
Printed and bound in Canada by Best Book Manufacturers
1 2 3 4 5   00 99 98 97 96

Production of this book is made possible by grants from the Canada Council and the
Cultural Services Branch, Province of British Columbia

CATALOGUING IN PUBLICATION DATA
    Williams, Judy, 1940-
    High slack

    (Transmontanus, ISSN 1200-3336; v. 4)
    Includes bibliographic references and index.
    ISBN 0-921586-45-0

    1. Homfray, Robert. 2. British Columbia – History – 1849-1871.* 3. Chilcotin Indians
– Wars. 4. Indians of North America – British Columbia – Wars. I. Title. II. Series.
FC3822.3.W44 1995   971.1'7502   C95-911021-6
F1088.W44 1995